D1075044

A BAPTIST MANUAL
of Polity and Practice

A BAPTIST MANUAL
of Polity and Practice

NORMAN H. MARING *and* WINTHROP S. HUDSON

JUDSON PRESS®
Valley Forge

Copyright © 1963

The Judson Press
Valley Forge, Pa.

The Bible quotations in this book are in accordance with the Revised Standard Version of the Bible, copyright 1946 and 1952 by the Division of Christian Education of the National Council of the Churches of Christ in the United States of America, and are used by permission.

Library of Congress Catalogue Card No. 62-18079

International Standard Book No. 0-8170-0299-5

Fourth Printing, 1981

The name JUDSON PRESS is registered
as a trademark in the U.S. Patent Office.

PRINTED IN THE U.S.A. ⊕

Contents

Foreword

MANY BAPTISTS HAVE LONG FELT THE NEED FOR A NEW BAPTIST "manual" that would bring together traditional Baptist positions and practices and the modifications adopted over the years by Baptists in local churches and in larger groupings. Baptist organization is not static. It changes slowly in keeping with the needs of people to maintain a vital and personal relationship between the individual and God through Jesus Christ. The gospel remains our basis, and the Baptist genius as exhibited in history is our guide. The application of these considerations, however, undergoes almost constant change which, while neither rapid nor cataclysmic, is none the less persistent. Baptists have always placed more emphasis on personal faith and experience than upon uniformity of structure or organization. Because of this very fact, it is almost axiomatic that varieties of practice should be found within the churches and among them.

The General Council of the American Baptist Convention several years ago initiated procedures which, it was hoped, would result in the production of a manual such as the one here presented. It was fully agreed that the manual could not bear an "official stamp of approval" in such a way as to be considered binding upon the churches or the Convention. Although it would be released only after having the constructive criticism of many groups and knowledgeable individuals, it would have to stand basically as the work of its authors themselves. It could take on an "official" stamp for Baptists in the only way any of its predecessors had: through acceptance and use over the years.

We feel deeply grateful in having secured the consent of two outstanding church historians to take the responsibility for writing this important document: Dr. Norman H. Maring, of Eastern Baptist Theological Seminary, and Dr. Winthrop S. Hudson, of the Colgate Rochester Divinity School. These two scholars know the great importance of historical handbooks in the development of Baptist thought and polity, and are quite aware of the process which brought these handbooks of the past into wide usage as "official" guides of faith and practice. A precise sense of historical perspective and value is the first requisite they have brought to this present task. But church historians occupied with the interpretation of history cannot live in the past. Dr. Maring and Dr. Hudson are thoroughly familiar with the modern scene. Their extensive studies of current procedures among our churches have qualified them fully to discharge their responsibilities of writing a new manual. They have sought and profited by the opinion of many others, but they bear full responsibility for the completed work.

Among those who have reviewed all or parts of the manuscript and have submitted written comments and criticisms of it are the Advisory Board for Theological Studies, the Executive Committee and most of the members of the Commission on the Ministry, the Executive Committees of American Baptist Men and the National Council of American Baptist Women, some members of the General Council, some officers of the Ministers Council, and selected staff members and leaders of the American Baptist Convention. Fully one hundred people in all have critically examined the manuscript. It must be obvious that the resulting criticisms and suggestions for change could not all be finally incorporated into the manual, for the simple reason that some were diametrically opposed to others. The authors have chosen the course of reviewing alternative views in connection with issues that have proven to be complex and persistently difficult for Baptists. They were greatly aided by the stimulating criticisms. These have led to modifications which, in their opinion, have strengthened the book as a whole and clarified many portions of it. The final product, while remaining that of Dr. Maring and Dr. Hudson, does reflect, to this extent, the judgment of those considered most capable in this field.

I commend this book to the thoughtful reading of all who would like to become more familiar with the people called "Baptists." Those responsible for leadership in local churches, associations and wider levels of organized witness and outreach will find this stimulating and provocative. It is hoped that many groups of Baptists at local, state, and national levels will make this work a subject of thoughtful inquiry and discussion.

Of course it is not the "final" word. Time alone will determine its proper place as far as an "official" expression of our policies and practices is concerned. One thing seems certain: Some future generation will feel the need for additional modifications in order to keep pace with the dynamic movement so evident among a people whose paramount desire is to enable man more fully to experience the power and presence of God in contemporary life.

EDWIN H. TULLER
General Secretary
American Baptist Convention

November 16, 1962

I

Identifying the Baptists

WHO ARE THE BAPTISTS? WHAT ARE THEIR CHARACTERISTIC BE-
liefs and practices? Numbering over twenty-five million persons, scattered around the world, and organized in many
separate bodies, they exhibit great variety. More than nine-
tenths of these Baptists are in the United States, but they are
divided into numerous groups based upon differences of
language, race, region, and doctrine. Even among the members of a single Baptist convention, there is wide latitude of
practice and teaching. In spite of the obvious differences
among Baptists, the fact that they bear a common name implies a common identity. What constitutes the core of Baptist
life and thought?

The attempt to define ourselves as Baptists is not an idle
pastime. The adherents of any Christian group need to know
who they are, what their purposes are, and what their role is,
for a group as well as an individual needs to understand itself.
To be confused about one's identity is demoralizing. If it is to
maintain its integrity in the midst of conflicting pressures, a
denomination needs to have a clear concept of itself. The
health and vitality of our denominational life depends upon
such clarity.

If self-definition is indispensable, it is also dangerous. In
seeking to define ourselves, we may overemphasize our dis-

1

tinctiveness. The search for clearer identity requires that we see ourselves in relationship to other Christians. It involves not only an understanding of our points of difference, but also of basic similarities. In the past we have been so preoccupied with defining our differences from other Christians that we have fostered a feeling of estrangement from them. It is a mistake to focus so much attention upon denominational "distinctives" that these obscure the more important elements which unite us as Christians.

1. SELF-DISCOVERY IN ECUMENICAL ENCOUNTER

Awareness of Christian Unity

The ecumenical movement which has flowered in our time has the great virtue of enabling us to experience the oneness of those who are in Christ. Brought face-to-face with Christians of diverse backgrounds, we learn to know them as kindred spirits who have also experienced the grace of our Lord Jesus Christ. Our eyes are opened to the unity which underlies our varieties of custom and thought. Moreover, we become aware of the need for a united Christian witness to the world. It would be wrong to stifle this sense of Christian unity by accentuating our differences.

The encounter with other Christians in the ecumenical movement has had a further healthy effect, for it has caused us to re-examine our denominational traditions. Not only are we invited to share a fellowship, but we are challenged to testify to our understanding of God's truth and listen to what others have to say. As a result of honest examination, our distinctive claims are discovered to be fewer and less important than we had supposed. Often we find that many of our apparent differences are more verbal than real.

Awareness of Particular Emphases

Points of agreement are important. But, having become aware that our agreements are more significant than our differences, we may be tempted to fall into the opposite error. In our eagerness to stress our common faith, we may brush aside all differences as of no consequence. Although many differences are due to misunderstanding, there are some disagreements which have practical significance for Christian faith and life. Differences of doctrine and practice should be subordinated to the central issue of faith in Jesus Christ as Lord and Savior. It does not follow, however, that all convictions concerning the gospel and the way in which it is communicated and appropriated should be ignored. Denominations exist because Christians must be faithful and obedient to God, in accord with the understandings to which he has led them.

Only as we are sure of our identity as Baptists can we participate responsibly within the larger church and share effectively in its witness to the world. Being clear about the heritage which we share with other Christian communions, we should also understand and appreciate the inheritance which we have as Baptists. With a clear conception of the characteristics of Baptist belief and life, we shall be in a better position to know which of those emphases are valid and relevant for today. Out of the integrity produced by greater self-understanding, we can play a more vigorous role within the church and be more articulate in addressing the need of the world.

The Role of Denominations

To share in fellowship through a denomination does not mean to be sectarian. No denomination has the right to claim that it alone is the "true church." It can declare that it has some insight which must not be overlooked, but it should be willing to examine such a claim candidly and submit it to the criticism of others within the Christian community. To recognize the inevitability of different interpretations is realistic. They spring from limitations of ignorance and sinfulness which are inherent within the human situation. So long as denominations can make it clear that their differences from other Christians are in matters of emphasis rather than in essential nature, they serve a legitimate and necessary purpose. They check the pretensions of one another, they keep alive facets of Christian truth which otherwise might be lost, and they remind us of the obligation to be true to the light which God has given to each of us.

2. SOME TYPICAL IDEAS ABOUT BAPTISTS

Confusion about Baptist Identity

What then should be rightfully identified as the characteristic marks of the Baptists? Who are we, and for what do we stand? There is no lack of answers to these questions in books and pamphlets about Baptists, but there is an embarrassing lack of agreement among the interpreters. Although we speak confidently of "the Baptist witness," "our Baptist heritage," or "the people called Baptists," there is some confusion regarding the substance of these terms. Too often statements have been made about our unique character which will not bear close examination. We have sometimes tried to explain ourselves with clichés and shibboleths which cause confusion instead of clarifying issues.

A typical list of Baptist distinctives is apt to include the following points: the Scriptures, or the New Testament, as the supreme authority for faith and practice; the priesthood of believers; freedom of conscience, soul liberty, and the right of private interpretation; congregational polity; the autonomy of the local church; believers' baptism by immersion; and a regenerate church membership. Some of them are not so much distinctive of Baptists as they are beliefs of Protestants in general. Others are distortions of some valid Baptist emphases. A few are closely related to the true genius of Baptists.

Some Typical Assertions about Baptists

In view of the fact that there is a large amount of confusion about Baptist identity, it is necessary to restudy our heritage to gain a clear picture of ourselves. For this purpose we shall first examine some of the tenets which Baptists commonly regard as distinctive of themselves, and then we shall review our Baptist beginnings to see how our forebears understood themselves.

There are many who believe that the uniqueness of Baptists is to be found in their loyalty to the Scriptures, but all Protestants affirm the Scriptures as their rule of faith and practice. Luther, Calvin, and the other Protestant Reformers vigorously asserted the authority of the Bible. In official doctrinal statements, such as *The Thirty-Nine Articles* of the Church of England and *The Westminster Confession* of the Church of Scotland and other Presbyterian bodies throughout the world, it is made clear that the Bible stands on a level above all creedal formulas and is normative for doctrine and life. Similar comments are applicable to "the priesthood of believers," a doctrine given classic formulation by Martin Luther.

It is frequently stated that the primary characteristic of Baptists is their love of liberty. "Soul liberty" and "the right of private judgment" are heralded as the special watchwords of the denomination. Although in our tradition there has been a cherished emphasis upon liberty of conscience, this has not always borne the same meaning which some modern interpreters give to it. Initially resting upon their belief in the sovereignty of God over the conscience, rather than upon human dignity and individual rights, early Baptists advocated a responsible freedom which had certain recognized limits. Today this doctrine of liberty is often taken to mean that each individual is free to adopt whatever views he will, without any restraints at all. Many Baptists thus take pride in their lack of agreement, boastfully asserting that where there are two Baptists there are at least three opinions. Early Baptists, however, would have regarded such a conception of freedom as unwarranted license, a view which can lead only to chaos. Thus, though liberty of conscience has been an important strand of Baptist tradition, the meaning of that concept today has been twisted beyond recognition.

For some people, the most prized doctrine of Baptists is "the autonomy of the local church." The notion of absolute independence of a local church, however, was foreign to the thinking of early Baptists. They adopted the congregational principle because they believed that it would afford the possibility of fuller obedience to God, who is the only Lord of the conscience. Especially in local affairs, such as the admission and exclusion of members and the choosing of a pastor, they needed to be free to ascertain and follow the will of the Lord. This right of "church power" represented a degree of independence, but it was balancd by a strong sense of *inter*dependence among congregations. Baptists recognized an obligation to maintain a wider fellowship, within which they would give assistance, accept counsel, and work toward common ends. Today there is a widespread misconception of this strand of Baptist ideology. In its original form it is essential to the Baptist genius, but the present-day idea of "absolute independence" creates misunderstanding and fosters anarchy.

Another characteristic of Baptist thought is the doctrine of the separation of church and state. This grows out of a conviction of the necessity for the church to be free to obey her Lord. While other Christians also believed that the Christian must be free to obey God, Baptists have asserted that such liberty was impeded by the activity of the civil government in religious affairs. Since they presupposed that only the elect could offer true worship to God, and that God alone could make himself known to these elect, they did not see how the state could have any part in matters of conscience. Therefore they insisted that the functions of political government should not include the enforcement of uniformity of worship and doctrine. The church, they said, must be left free to seek and to execute the will of God. Happily, this is a view that is now shared by most American Protestants.

The most important difference between Baptists and other Protestants is widely believed to be the practice of baptism by immersion. An average person, being asked about Baptist emphases, would probably mention this as a chief distinctive. Without minimizing the importance of immersion as a form of baptism, it must be said that this is not the primary mark of differentiation. Most informed Baptists would protest that the mode of baptism is not the chief distinction of their denomination. Indeed, the earliest Baptists seem to have baptized by pouring water upon the head rather than by immersion.[1]

Much closer to the heart of Baptist concern is "believers' baptism"—the restriction of baptism to persons who make a personal profession of faith. From both a theological and a practical point of view, this practice is significant. In the first place, Baptists believe that New Testament baptism signifies faith and repentance, and therefore it is to be administered only to those who are old enough to make responsible decisions. At the same time, by confining baptism to persons who have made personal professions of faith, the churches guard the entrance to membership and try to maintain regenerate churches. In so doing, they come close to the original emphasis which called the Baptists into existence.

The Need for More Adequate Definitions

This survey of Baptist self-interpretations makes it clear that more precise and more adequate self-definition is needed. Some current statements have distorted our tradition. Others indicate that the passage of time has blurred our image of ourselves. If we are to recover an understanding of ourselves, we must once again look at our historical roots. We may ask how the Baptists originated. Against what were they reacting? What were they concerned to protect? What were their chief concerns? A view of ourselves in the perspective of our historical beginnings will afford a vantage point for better understanding who we are as Baptists.

3. A LOOK AT BAPTIST ORIGINS

The Importance of Locating Origins

Serious students will recognize that historical investigation is not simply an antiquarian pursuit, although some people see

[1] R. G. Torbet, *A History of the Baptists, Revised Edition*, pages 42-43. Valley Forge: The Judson Press, 1963.

little value in a study of the past. We are living in the present, some people say, and do not need to find out what our ancestors may have done. A knowledge of history, however, can be of great practical importance, and the reconstruction of the situation out of which Baptists emerged can contribute to our self-understanding. For only when we have settled the question about our beginnings shall we be in a position to find clues to many of the questions pertaining to Baptist tradition. When we have ascertained the historical point at which Baptists came into being, the groups with which they were associated, and the issues on which they separated, we shall be able to see how they viewed their own significance. Not only will we see what they considered to be their distinguishing marks, but we may also learn much about the theology and practices of our early Baptist predecessors.

Theories of Baptist Origins

Historians have sometimes differed in locating these Baptist beginnings, but it seems clear today that our denomination had its origin within English congregationalism. Although there is a widely circulated notion that Baptist churches have had an unbroken succession from the first century, there is no reason to give credence to such a fanciful theory. Historical evidence does not support the idea that a chain of Christian churches with definite Baptist traits has existed apart from the main stream of Christianity. Such an outward succession, even if it existed, would be irrelevant to the Baptist understanding of the church. Even an assertion of spiritual kinship between Baptists and a wide variety of schismatic and heretical groups over the centuries is meaningless. To try to establish special relationships between Baptists and assorted movements in the early centuries necessitates the ignoring of important differences and is bound to be misleading. On such a basis one could even claim a special affinity between Mormons and Baptists, different as they are, since both practice immersion. By such a process some Buddhists in Taiwan have asserted that Henry

Wadsworth Longfellow (a Unitarian) was a Buddhist, because he once was so remorseful over shooting a bird that he never again carried a gun!

Another popular view connects Baptists with the Anabaptists, particularly with a Mennonite group in Holland. Although there are some similarities between Baptist and Mennonite doctrines, there are also great points of contrast. Moreover, no direct connection has been traced which would link Baptist origins to a Mennonite source.

Baptist Relationship to Puritanism

There is really no necessity to look beyond the English scene in order to account for Baptist origins, for they were a natural outgrowth in the evolution of English Puritanism. If we wish to see Baptist beginnings in their proper setting, it is necessary to retrace the rather obvious stages by which they arose out of the Puritan background. At its inception, Puritanism was a reform movement within the Church of England. Having expected a thorough housecleaning in the Church of England, some leaders were disappointed when Queen Elizabeth seemed only to have swept the dirt under the rug. Therefore they sought to reform that church according to the Word of God, and their program called for the removal of certain practices reminiscent of what they called "popery." Objections were raised to much of the ritual of the Book of Common Prayer and to the wearing of special garb at the Lord's Supper. As the movement developed, its aims were expanded to include a demand that a presbyterian system of church government be substituted for the episcopal polity. The authority of bishops would then be transferred to the presbyterial organizations of the churches.

Although these Puritans stood for a deepened spiritual life in the churches, they did not reject two important assumptions which were almost universally held in Europe. First, they expected everyone in a given geographical area to be a member of the parish church. Thus, they had no objection to laws requiring that all infants be baptized. Second, they acknowledged the right of the civil ruler to supervise the life of the church. In their view it was the duty of the state to support and protect the church by wise legislation, by financial support, and by the suppression of heresy. In both of these views the Puritan outlook accorded with that of the Church of England, as well as with those of the Roman Catholics and most Protestants in Europe.

Out of the Puritan wing of the Anglican Church, there developed a congregational party which did not accept the idea that everyone automatically belongs to the church. Rejecting the concept of the "parish church" with its mixed multitude of believers and unbelievers, the leaders of this wing of the Puritan movement declared that visible churches ought to be composed of "visible saints." They insisted that churches should admit to membership only those persons who could testify to their own Christian experience. With membership thus restricted, congregations were transformed into "gathered" instead of "parish" congregations. Having covenanted to form a congregation, the members of each church became responsible for governing their own affairs.

Having taken this step, however, the early advocates of congregationalist principles still stopped short of pursuing their basic contention to its logical conclusion. Although they wished to limit church membership to believers, they were reluctant to exclude children completely. Thus, they retained baptism for the children of the church members, and said that the churches are composed of visible saints "and their children." It was expected, of course, that when these children grew up they would be able to testify to God's saving work in their lives. They would then be admitted to the Lord's Table and to full membership. When the children thus baptized became adults, however, many of them were unable to testify to any experience of conversion. The presence of such persons who had been baptized, but had been unable to qualify for full membership in the church, was embarrassing. This situation led some to conclude that the practice of infant baptism was inconsistent with the idea of a "gathered" church. Dissatisfaction also arose at another point. The congregationalist party still adhered to the idea that the civil government was responsible for the welfare of the church. Although they claimed the right to withdraw from the Church of England, they hoped for a day when they would enjoy state support as the official faith. It soon became apparent to some, however, that this position was also inconsistent.

Those who advocated a clean break with the Church of England were dubbed Separatists. There were others who held a congregational theory, but were loath to secede from the Church of England. The former group furnished the Pilgrim settlers who eventually founded the settlement at Plymouth in 1620, whereas the latter started the Massachusetts Bay Colony in 1630. In the New World both groups found opportunity to translate their theories into practice, unhampered by the civil government or the older church.

In the rise of a people with congregationalist sentiments may be seen a movement which reached the very brink of adopting principles which would have made them Baptists. In the ferment of religious ideas in the seventeenth century, it is not surprising that some persons decided to take the next step. Consistent adherence to the gathered-church principle required the rejection of infant baptism and of the state church concept. When people were ready to take these two steps, the Baptists arrived on the scene.

Origin from English Congregationalism Illustrated

In some cases Baptists emerged from Separatists; in other instances their background was that of non-separating Congregationalists. In many ways the Baptists continued to resemble Congregationalists. They maintained the idea of the "gathered church," and they emphasized the importance of the local church in the government of its own affairs. *At only two important points did the Baptists take a different line: namely, by insisting that believers' baptism was necessary to the gathered-church idea, and by advocating the freedom of churches from the control of civil government.*

The first illustration of the transition from Congregationalist to Baptist principles is found in a Separatist congregation which had fled from England to Amsterdam.[2] When the pastor, John Smyth, concluded that infant baptism was wrong, and persuaded the congregation of the correctness of his views, the church was reconstituted upon a basis of believers' baptism. Smyth baptized himself and then baptized the others. Smyth also was convinced that a church which is responsible to Christ as its head must have freedom from ecclesiastical and civil interference. This conviction led him to publish one of the earliest defences of liberty of conscience.

Shortly after Smyth had baptized himself and his congregation, he learned of a local Mennonite church which already practiced believers' baptism. Beginning to doubt the propriety of his self-baptism, he began to make overtures to the Mennonites which might lead to a rebaptism and perhaps union with them. Some members of his congregation, however, saw no reason to question the validity of their baptism by Smyth. When their pastor persisted in his negotiations with the Dutch Mennonites, this group, led by Thomas Helwys, returned to England. In 1612, they formed the first Baptist church on English soil.

These first Baptists had been affected by current theological discussions about human freedom, and they adopted some positions which were not approved by most contemporary Calvinists. They asserted that the atonement of Christ was sufficient to save all men, not just the elect. Because of their ad-

[2] It is of interest to observe in passing that the members of this church had been closely associated in England with a Separatist congregation of which John Robinson was the pastor. Both of these groups fled to Holland, where one took a route which led its members to become founders of New England Congregationalism at Plymouth, and the other followed a course which resulted in their becoming Baptists. This connection serves to show how closely connected Baptists and Congregationalists were in this early period.

herence to this concept of a general atonement, they were called General Baptists. Although this group experienced some growth during the seventeenth century, it dwindled after 1700, and never had much influence upon the mainstream of Baptist development. It is important for our purpose to note that these Baptists limited baptism to those who had made a profession of faith and rejected all interference by the civil government. Thus they were differentiated from the Congregationalist party.

A second instance of Baptist beginnings, unrelated to that of the Smyth group, came about in 1638. Several people withdrew from a Congregationalist church in London to form a new church on the basis of believers' baptism. The parent church had been Congregationalist in its emphasis upon the concept of a gathered church, but it had shied away from complete separation from the Church of England. Sharing the general theological outlook of the non-separating Congregationalists, these Baptists were more typical Calvinists than were the General Baptists. Holding the doctrine of a "particular" atonement (Christ having died only for the elect), they were known as Particular Baptists. Living in almost complete isolation from each other, the General and Particular Baptists developed in different ways. It was the latter who eventually represented the main line of Baptist history in England and in America. The traits which these groups had in common, and which distinguished them from their fellow Dissenters, were the practice of believers' baptism and a specific theory of religious liberty.

The third case of an independent Baptist beginning is of less moment for subsequent Baptist history, but it illustrates again the ease with which Congregationalist views could lead to a Baptist position. In this instance the leading spirit was Roger Williams. Having moved from being a moderate Puritan to a strong Separatist, he denied the right of civil government to interfere in matters of conscience at all. Expelled from the Massachusetts Bay settlement, he established a new colony, where in 1639 he joined with others to form a church on the basis of believers' baptism. He himself was associated with the Baptist church at Providence for only a few weeks, and the Providence church exercised little influence upon the spread and development of the Baptist cause in America. Once more, however, it may be seen how Baptists emerged logically and naturally out of the Congregationalist setting by refusing to baptize infants and by affirming the freedom of the church from the authority of the state.

4. HISTORIC BAPTIST EMPHASES

Baptists were not sectarian. This excursion into Baptist origins should enable us to recognize more clearly both the common heritage which Baptists shared with others and the points which distinguished them. From what the early Baptists wrote and did, it is plain that most of them were not sectarians. This fact was notably true of the Particular Baptists. They did not cut themselves off from fellowship with other Christians, nor did they feel that they had an exclusive claim to truth. That they regarded themselves as Protestants is indicated in many statements, and their close kinship with Presbyterians and Congregationalists is reflected in early confessions of faith.

Characteristic Baptist Emphases

The doctrine of the church is where the Baptists began to diverge from other Protestants. Indeed, a modern Baptist historian has asserted that "the distinctive feature about Baptists is their doctrine of the church."[3] It was not the nature and mission of the church which provided the point of disagreement; rather, Baptists differed with their fellow-Protestants concerning the way in which the church finds visible expression and does its work in the world. Even at this point they had much in common with early Congregationalists.

Like the Congregationalists, Baptists believed that the visible churches should approximate the invisible by maintaining a re-

[3] W. T. Whitley, *A History of British Baptists,* page 4. Philadelphia: J. B. Lippincott, 1923.

generate membership. The Baptists added, however, that such gathered churches are possible only when the door to membership is guarded by baptizing exclusively persons who have made a personal profession of faith. It is this view that regenerate churches can be realized only in conjunction with believers' baptism which distinguished Baptists in the beginning. Like the Congregationalists, the Baptists believed that each local congregation had power from Christ to govern its own affairs, but the Baptists early developed the associational principle to give visible expression to the interdependence of local churches. The other point at which Baptists differed from Congregationalists was in their insistence upon complete separation between spheres of church and state. *In summary, then, we may say that the distinguishing marks of the Baptists, historically speaking, were: a regenerate membership safeguarded by believers' baptism; congregational polity, coupled with an associational principle; and the necessity of freeing the church from interference by the civil government.*

We began this chapter by asking: Who are the Baptists? It is easier to answer the question: Who were the Baptists? It should, however, be of some help to know where we began. Knowing where we started, we may trace the path by which we have traveled; we may see what alterations have been made, either deliberately or unconsciously. We are then in a better position to judge whether or not the changes have been justified.

An understanding of the way in which early Baptists viewed themselves also helps us rid ourselves of false notions about our distinctiveness. As indicated earlier, some Baptists have preempted general Protestant teachings and claimed to make them peculiarly Baptist. This has often led to an exaggerated sense of uniqueness and has contributed to isolation and provincialism. Indeed when we consider the situation today, the area of disagreement has been narrowed considerably. At the present time, congregational ideas, the conception of regenerate membership, and the ideal of religious liberty have permeated

American Christianity. Therefore it is questionable whether there is any value in using the term "distinctive," which unduly enhances the idea of differences and encourages too much separateness. There are certain emphases which Baptists have historically championed, and they will do well to continue to witness to the importance of these through their own teaching and practice.

Before we proceed to a further discussion of the Baptist doctrine of the church and to assess its worth for today, it is necessary to devote a chapter to the biblical doctrine of the church. In order to make decisions we need criteria of judgment, and for us the biblical view of the church must be our norm.

II

The New Testament Concept
of the Church

THE SEARCH FOR A CLEARER SENSE OF BAPTIST IDENTITY IS NOT
ended when we have uncovered our historical antecedents.
It is still necessary to ask whether the distinguishing ideas of
our fathers are still important. If not, we need not perpetuate
them. On the other hand, if they still testify in significant ways
to the gospel of Christ, then we must continue to cherish them.

1. THE NEED FOR A DOCTRINE OF THE CHURCH

Baptist Ecclesiology: Is It Adequate?

The distinctive character of Baptist life, as we have learned,
springs from a particular understanding of the church. The
question which we must now face is whether that understanding is true, adequate, and significant. Is the historic conception of church polity and practice appropriate for our day?

By what tests of adequacy, then, are we to answer this
question? History can show us how Baptists organized to express their faith, but it cannot furnish criteria for judging the
adequacy of such views. Nor can practical needs be the chief
guide in judging a church polity. When expediency becomes
the primary consideration in determining its form and program,
the essential character of the church may be obscured. There

17

is also a perpetual risk that the desire to achieve influence as an institution may lead the church to deny its own nature. Therefore, although both history and practical considerations should be taken into account, the ultimate standard must be theological. In other words, all church order must grow out of an understanding of the nature and mission of the church, and should be so designed as to fulfill God's purpose for it. Moreover, such an understanding of the church can only be derived in any ultimate sense from the Scriptures which testify to God's intention in Christ.

Thus, our question about Baptist identity leads to the biblical doctrine of the church. Having begun by asking who the Baptists are, we must now come to a prior question, namely: What is the New Testament concept of the church? Before one can proceed far in the discussion of polity and practice, he must have some answer to this prior question. For out of our concept of the church will come deductions as to matters of practice. Our next step, then, is to inquire about the church as it is depicted in the Scriptures. We shall then be in a better position to examine traditional Baptist ideas to see whether they are in accord with this biblical portrayal.

A High View of the Church

The doctrine of the church is a matter of vital importance. After years of neglect, Baptists as well as other Protestants are rediscovering how crucial is the place of the church in God's redemptive purpose. Unawareness of the divine dimensions of the church has often led us to treat it as an institution which could be explained in sociological terms alone. An inadequate conception of the church encourages members to be careless about their responsibilities, to attend its services when convenient, and to give leftovers of money and energies.

When a low view of the church is held by those within its ranks, it is natural that the world should have a similar estimate of its worth. Although the little volume by C. S. Lewis, *The Screwtape Letters,* is fantasy, there is truth in Satan's mes-

sage to his emissary, Wormwood. Having chided his underling
for allowing his human charge to become converted, Satan
then consoled him with the hope that the man might return
when he found out what churches are like: "One of our great
allies at present is the Church itself. Do not misunderstand me.
I do not mean the Church as we see her spread out through all
time and space and rooted in eternity, terrible as an army with
banners. That, I confess, is a spectacle which makes our boldest
tempters uneasy."[1] There can be no doubt that we often treat
the church as though it were of second-rate importance. The
weakened impact of the church upon the world today is par-
tially due to the fact that Christians have had an inadequate
understanding of its role. Therefore, it is a hopeful sign that we
are coming to accept the high view which the New Testament
has of the church of Christ.

2. THE BIBLICAL DOCTRINE OF THE CHURCH

To recover the biblical teaching about the church is not as
easy as it might seem. The fact that in our usage we assign several meanings to the same word "church" enhances the difficulty of defining it. When we speak of "the church on the cor-
ner," we are likely to mean a building. Again, the word may be
used to refer to a worship service, when one remarks, "I am
staying for church today." We speak of the Episcopal Church
or the Presbyterian Church, and thereby we designate a denomination. At other times, our conversation may include some
mention of "our church," and thus we signify a local congregation. The same term is employed to speak of the universal
church of the past and present, the totality of believers. It is
little wonder that there is confusion about the word "church."

What then does "church" mean? What is its meaning in the
New Testament? When we turn to find an answer to this ques-
tion, we are faced with a number of secondary problems. Did
Jesus found the church? When was the church founded—when

[1] C. S. Lewis, *The Screwtape Letters*, page 15. New York: The Macmillan
Company, 1943.

Jesus chose the Twelve? at the Last Supper? at Pentecost? Did the church exist prior to the Incarnation? What is the connection between the Israel of the Old Testament and the church of the New Testament? Is the kingdom of God preached by Jesus the same as the church? What is the relationship between the church and the churches? Is the local church primary, and the concept of a universal church an abstraction, derived from adding together all of the local congregations? Or is the universal church primary, and each local congregation an expression of it? All of these subsidiary questions are involved in the discussion of the church.

If one expects to find in the New Testament a concise passage which describes the nature of the church, he will be disappointed. At first, there was no one standardized term by which the Christian community was designated. It was referred to by equivalent terms, such as brethren, the way, assembly, family, household, people, body, etc. It was not until later that the term *ecclesia* (meaning, in its broad sense, a "calling out" or "assembly," and translated "church" in the English versions of the Bible), came to be accepted as the standard term. There is no special reason why a word meaning "people" or "household" could not have been adopted instead. Certainly such words occur frequently in the New Testament. It is necessary for us to get behind these varied terms and to uncover their common underlying assumptions if we are to arrive at a clear understanding of the nature and purpose of the church.

In the following discussion, we shall approach our question from three directions. First, we shall look at the message of Jesus to see its implications for the church. Second, the letter to the Ephesians will be summarized to get a Pauline view of the church. Third, the relationship between the church and the "people of God" of the Old Testament will be noted.

Jesus and the Church

Since there were various terms in the Greek language for the reality we now call the church, it is not surprising that only one of the four Gospels uses the specific word *ecclesia*. It is mentioned only in Matthew 16:18 and 18:17, and in the second of these places it seems to be referring to the synagogue. The fact that Jesus seldom employed the term has led some interpreters to infer that he had no intention of establishing the church. Some New Testament scholars of the past fifty years have declared the church was a later invention of Jesus' disciples. This interpretation, however, is to mistake a word for the reality. It is now clear to biblical scholars that he expected to establish a people who should bear his name and continue his work.

The terms which Jesus used expressed his expectation that a community of disciples would succeed him, and the major part of his ministry was directed to the preparation of a company of men who would continue his mission. The two synonymous phrases, "the kingdom of God" and "the kingdom of heaven," implied the creation of a community or fellowship. The emphasis in these terms is not so much upon a temporal kingdom as upon men's relationship to the sovereign rule of God. To proclaim the kingdom was to bid men to accept God's rule, to enter his fellowship, to receive his saving power, and to yield their lives in obedient service. The sovereign God announced by Jesus was a father who invited men to accept his forgiveness and become his children; as his children, these men would become brothers. Thus the kingdom announced by Jesus was a new set of relationships, vertical and horizontal. It was a community between man and God and between man and man, which was being proclaimed by Jesus Christ and created through the power of the Holy Spirit. Inaugurated by the messianic ministry of Jesus, the kingdom was present then, but not in its fullness. It had a future aspect—beyond history—when the kingdom would be consummated.

What Jesus did was to establish a community of persons who were united by their loyalty to him and by the indwelling of God's power. Other terms which he employed pointed to the same close-knit fellowship, as when he referred to his followers as "little flock" (Luke 12:32), "my mother and my brothers"

(Luke 8:21), or "the branches" (John 15:5). The creation of this community was a primary object of his earthly ministry. It appears that he gave surprisingly little attention to institutional forms. He left no written instructions; he developed no elaborate system of ritual. What he left was a fellowship of men who had been convinced that Jesus was the long-awaited Messiah in whom God had uniquely manifested himself to men, once for all.

The purpose of this community was to carry on the ministry which Jesus had begun. To his disciples Jesus stated their mission in these words: "As the Father has sent me, even so I send you" (John 20:21). At the close of the Matthean Gospel is given the Great Commission: "Go therefore and make disciples of all nations, baptizing them in the name of the Father and of the Son and of the Holy Spirit, teaching them to observe all that I have commanded you; and lo, I am with you always, to the close of the age" (Matt. 28:19-20). The phrase "the extension of the incarnation" is sometimes used to describe the mission of the church, but it makes too close an identification between Christ and the church. We must beware of any figure which might convey the idea that the church in its sinfulness is one and the same with Jesus Christ, its head. It is better to express the work of the church by saying that it is intended to carry on the ministry of Christ in preaching, teaching, and serving.

Paul's Letter to the Ephesians

The clearest exposition of the nature and purpose of the church is Paul's letter to the Ephesians. Against the background of a world deeply involved in evil, the writer portrays the church as a body which has a redemptive mission. A summary of the Ephesian letter will help to bring the New Testament doctrine of the church into focus.

"Blessed be . . . God," begins the author, " . . . for he has made known to us . . . the mystery of his will, according to his purpose which he set forth in Christ" (Eph. 1:3, 9). That eternal purpose, hitherto a secret, has now been revealed—namely, that God intends to "unite all things in [Christ]" (1:10). In the life, death, resurrection, and exaltation of Jesus Christ, God has invaded human history and in principle has defeated the power of sin and death. Having completed his mighty acts of redemption in Jesus Christ, he now continues to work in this divided, sin-sick world by the Spirit, through the church which is "his body" (1:23).

Indeed, the writer of the letter asserts, the process of uniting all things has already begun with the reconciliation of Jew and Gentile. By the same power with which God raised Christ from the dead, he has also made us alive with Christ (2:1). He has "broken down the dividing wall of hostility" (2:14) between two elements of the population. In order to "create in himself one new man in place of the two" (2:15), he has reconciled Jew and Gentile to God. Thus, God is creating a new humanity, and for this purpose the church has been called into being.

The "therefore" of Ephesians 4:1 reminds the readers again that they have been chosen by God, made alive with Christ, set apart to "live for the praise of his glory" (1:12), and to make known "the manifold wisdom of God" to all the universe (3:10). "I therefore," appeals Paul, ". . . beg you to lead a life worthy of the calling to which you have been called." In effect, he is urging the church to be the church! He wants the people of God to be clear about their identity and their mission, to know what God has called them to be and to do. God's call to the church is a call to unity and holiness, so that her life will be a persuasive witness to the world.

The rest of the letter deals with some specific ways in which the church can fulfill the vocation to which God has called her. The ministry belongs to the entire church and not just to a special ministerial class. Some special gifts, to be sure, have been bestowed for leadership in the church, but this leadership is provided "for the equipment of the saints for the work of the ministry, for the building up of the body of Christ" (4:11-12).[2] Led and informed by those who are endowed with special gifts and appointed to offices in the church, the whole body is to grow up, "until we all attain to the unity of the faith and of the knowledge of the Son of God, to mature manhood, to the measure of the stature of the fulness of Christ" (4:13).

Furthermore, the instructions of the last three chapters of Ephesians indicate that our ministry as members of Christ's body, the church, involves a many-sided witness. Love is to be expressed in all of our human relationships. Personal integrity is demanded ("putting away falsehood," "no longer steal," etc.). Relationships in the home (husband-wife, parent-child) and at work (servant-master) are to be brought under the lordship of Christ. The church witnesses not only by what it says, but by what it is. Through the depth of its fellowship, the Christian community is to make clear the power of God which makes for unity ("eager to maintain the unity of the Spirit in the bond of peace," 4:3).

Thus God works in and through the church, which is the body of Christ. As the relationships and quality of life within the Christian community express love, unity, and dedication, the Holy Spirit uses the church to fulfill God's purpose to unite all things in Christ. The practical implications of this letter are many, and call for a church different from much of the institutional life which characterizes the churches today.

The Church as the Israel of God

The letter which the apostle Paul wrote to the Ephesians makes explicit a conception of the church that is implicit throughout the Bible. It is important, therefore, to see this idea as it appears within the context of the whole biblical record. Throughout the Old and New Testaments run certain motifs

[2] The comma after "saints," which appears in the KJV and the RSV is not a part of the original text. See the translation of J. B. Phillips and *The New English Bible*, which omit it. The insertion of the comma obscures the meaning of the statement.

which give unity to the record, and these furnish a framework in which the church must be understood. The first of these primary themes is that of God as creator; another is that of man whom Pascal called "the glory and the scandal of the universe." Made in the divine image and endowed with freedom and responsibility, man has persistently misused that freedom in revolt against the will of his maker. To the conception of God as creator, then, is added that of redeemer, as he seeks to win men to acknowledge his divine sovereignty and to find their fulfillment in him. Thus begin the parallel strands of the biblical narrative: man as a sinner unwilling to accept his status as a creature, and God as the redeemer whose mercy is everlasting.

The story of God's purpose to redeem man from alienation and bondage to sin is connected in the Old Testament with a particular people. The history of Israel, the corporate name given to the people chosen for this special mission, became the history of God's redemptive work. Speaking to them through his mighty acts, God welded them into a nation which had a consciousness of being called for a divine mission. To this people with whom he made a covenant, God spoke repeatedly in judgment and mercy, in warning and promise. Eventually, however, Israel refused to fulfill its vocation, and God finally rejected her. Only a remnant was left, and that remainder was represented in the person of the Messiah.

In the New Testament the story of God's redemptive purpose continues, centering in the person of Jesus the Messiah, who called to himself a people in whom God's purpose would be realized. Thus, Israel was reconstituted; the church of Jesus Christ became the new Israel of God, the people of the new covenant. That re-creation of Israel in the church was taking place when Jesus called the Twelve, reminiscent of the twelve tribes of Israel, and when he instituted the Lord's Supper which signified the new covenant ratified by his blood. However, it was only after the crucifixion, resurrection, and exaltation that the messianic work was completed and a new power was released. Then came Pentecost, when, in the fullest sense, the Israel of God was re-established in the form of the Christian church.

That the church considered itself the heir of Israel's vocation as God's chosen people is attested in many passages. In the letter to the Galatians, for example, Paul speaks of the church as "the Israel of God" (6:16). In the same epistle he wrote: "It is men of faith who are the sons of Abraham" (3:7). To the Romans he said: "Not all who are descended from Israel belong to Israel . . . but the children of the promise are reckoned as descendants" (Romans 9:6, 8). The same idea is addressed to Christians in 1 Peter: "But you are a chosen race, a royal priesthood, a holy nation, God's own people, that you may declare the wonderful deeds of him who called you" (1 Peter 2:9). Here in unmistakable language it may be seen that the early church regarded itself as closely identified with the old Israel and the inheritor of its promises and responsibilities.

Against the background of this holy history, the features of the church stand out in clearer outline, and the relationship of the church to the total purpose of God is thrown into sharp relief. The church is then seen to be no afterthought of the apostles, no mere interim makeshift to fill a stopgap in the present age. It is the nucleus of the kingdom of God, the realm of redemption, the agency in and through which God accomplishes his purpose for the world.

Although this connection between the old and the new Israel needs to be stressed, we should not forget that there is more than simple continuity here. There are differences as well as resemblances. What had been a vaguely defined hope was now fulfilled. Instead of peering with hopeful eyes into a dim future, the new Israel could look back to recall what God had done in Christ. Under the New Covenant, the establishment of the people of God no longer was based upon birthright, but upon personal response. There was a new emphasis upon inwardness and depth in the requirements of those who became the disciples of Jesus Christ.

3. SOME CONCLUSIONS REGARDING THE CHURCH

The Nature of the Church

Several conclusions may be drawn from this discussion of the church. In the first place, the church is a people. Early Baptists sought to remind themselves of this fact by calling the places in which they met "meeting houses." The word "church" was reserved to apply to men and women in the divine-human fellowship. Our varied use of the term "church," however, makes us lose sight of this fact and makes it apply to something impersonal. An experience with an overseas student in a seminary provides a forceful illustration of this tendency. Having become acquainted with a certain congregation, he asked the pastor if he could get a picture of the church to take home with him. The minister said that he would take care of it later. After the service, when the congregation had dispersed, the pastor said that now they could take a picture of the church. "But," protested the student, "how can we take a picture of the church? The people have gone home!"

Secondly, not only is the church a people, but it is the people *of God*. The phrase "people of God" is synonymous with "the church of God" or "assembly of God." Indeed wherever the word "church" is used in the New Testament, the words "of God" are implied when they are not expressed. The church is not simply a voluntary association of good men who have banded themselves together to help God. Although their human response to God's gracious offer is not to be denied, the divine initiative is of first importance. It is God who has *called* the church into being.

The third point to be drawn from the discussion is that the church is to be seen as a close-knit fellowship, not simply a collection of loosely-related individuals. Indeed, one of the most impressive terms by which the inner meaning of the church is expressed in the New Testament is "fellowship" *(koinonia)*. Fellowship is not simply something which the church sometimes enjoys; the church *is* a fellowship. Prof. Emil

Brunner has emphasized that fact by saying that the church is "nothing other than a fellowship of persons."[3] In our common usage, the word "fellowship" has been debased, so that it means the good times we enjoy when there is a church supper or gathering for recreation. In the New Testament, however, "fellowship" signifies participation in the divine life and power, a life which is characterized by sharing. Beginning with the sharing which man experiences in the salvation of God, it goes on to include sharing the good news with others and even sharing one's property. The church then *is* a fellowship, or community, a participation in the life of the Spirit.

Another way of reiterating this idea is to insist that the church is not simply a means to an end, not a crutch to assist individual growth. To consider the church in that way is the same as to say that the family exists only in order to assist the development of individuals. The relationships which make up family life are important in themselves. The individual self becomes a real person in relationship with others, and his selfhood is intricately involved in a complex network of interrelationships. Likewise, the individual Christian cannot rightly be severed from the context of the Christian community. The individual is important, of course, and the fellowship is important, but they are inextricably intertwined. It is a mistake to try to separate them and to make one simply an instrument for the development of the other.

In the fourth place, the church acknowledges Jesus Christ as its Lord. He is "the head of the church," wrote Paul (Eph. 5:23), identifying the church itself as Christ's body. The heart of the apostolic preaching centers upon Jesus as God's promised Messiah whose life, death, resurrection, and exaltation have ultimate significance for man's redemption. Not only do his remembered teachings furnish guidance for the life of the church, but the Holy Spirit makes him present as its living Lord. His will supersedes all human claims.

[3] Emil Brunner, *The Misunderstanding of the Church,* page 10. Philadelphia: Westminster Press, 1953.

The Mission of the Church

Further, this close-knit community gathered by God is called to be a *servant* people. If it becomes so preoccupied with analyzing its own nature and conducting its internal affairs, that it forgets its mission to the world, it ceases to be the church. As the body of Christ, the church is the sphere in which God's Spirit operates in a special way; through this body, God's presence and power are communicated. The Christian community represents the demonstration project in this world of what can be done through God's power. It is the spearhead of God's reconciling movement. Here is the place where God is creating that "one new humanity" out of discordant elements, a community in which the barriers which separate men are removed. By what it *does*, what it *says*, and what it *is* the church proclaims the grace of God which makes men alive and incorporates them into the new society. It is thus a people called to worship, witness, teach, and serve in the name of Christ.

Worship, first of all, is an indispensable part of the life of the church. Called "to live for the praise of his glory," (Eph. 1:12) the church is bidden to sing "psalms and hymns and spiritual songs . . . making melody to the Lord with all your heart." (5:19). Although ritual may easily drift into mere formalism, yet the use of such rites serves an important purpose in keeping the church in vital touch with Christ. As branches must remain in connection with the vine, so must the Christian fellowship keep closely related with the source of its life. Unless there is constant renewal of the sense of God's presence and power, there will be no spiritual resources for ministering to the world. The church must continually offer itself in gratitude to God, and from God it must receive renewal of faith and power, if it is to be the bearer of revelation and a redemptive fellowship.

Secondly, the church is also called to be a witnessing community. Its responsibility for evangelism is so clear that there should be no need to remind Christians of it. The fact that

God makes use of the church in the realization of his redemptive purpose indicates the words "church" and "evangelism" are inseparably connected. The entire church is included in the commission to witness to the world, although not everyone shares in the same way in this ministry of reconciliation.

Unfortunately, for many people the word "evangelism" is associated with sensational methods and an atmosphere charged with emotion. Evangelism means essentially the outreach of the church to persuade men to acknowledge Jesus Christ as Savior and to obey him as Lord in the totality of their lives. In this sense, missions and evangelism have the same meaning. They are not to be identified with particular methods of winning men to Christ, for methods vary with time and place. The point which needs to be emphasized is that evangelistic witness is integral to the life of the church. We must seek the most effective means of communicating with a world which is being attracted by secularism, revolutionary nationalism, and communism. For this kind of witness we must learn how to live as Christians in the common life of our workaday world, in the home, in the community, in the sphere of the intellect, and in our churches. Whatever the method or the occasion, the church is called to be a witnessing fellowship.

In the third place, the church is called to be a ministering community. Actually, no clear lines can be drawn between the church's witness and its service. By our concern for others and our ministry to their need, we witness to the love of God and seek to point men to Christ. For purposes of analysis we may distinguish between evangelism and service, but in reality we witness by what we are and what we do as well as by what we say.

To call Christ Lord is to accept his claims upon our lives and to acknowledge that we are his servants. In the New Testament, the servant role of the church is emphasized by the figure of stewardship. The image of a steward stresses that we are not our own, but are God's. We are dependent upon God for our very lives, and our abilities and possessions are entrusted to us for temporary use. To accept the lordship of Christ over the church is to imply that all of life is to be lived under the direction of the one who is its head. Somehow, then, the church must learn to live responsibly with regard to the world and its needs; it cannot bypass social issues of our times as the Levite ignored the suffering man on the road to Jericho. Christ has bidden his disciples not only to love God, but to manifest that love by a sense of responsible concern towards those whom he has given to be our neighbors, whether the neighbor next door or the one on the other side of the world.

Finally, the church must teach if it is to live. Failure to teach produces weak churches which can hardly be distinguished from the world. Only as the Christian community understands its nature and mission can it maintain its identity. Its values, its ideals, and the power of God must therefore be transmitted to each generation, not just as a set of ideas, but as attitudes and loyalties essential for carrying out its role.

To be faithful in its teaching, the church has to take a serious interest in theology. If Christianity were simply a matter of emotions, we could dispense with the attempt to develop a fairly consistent theological rationale. But a firm faith requires the total commitment of the whole person, where heart and mind are in accord. Theology is the backbone of religion; it steadies and stiffens it. Without it, Christianity grows flabby and sentimental, and finally becomes laden with superstition.

Therefore, the church must accept responsibility to teach its members. It must formulate its own convictions in order to instruct the children and youth committed to its care. It must enable members to develop criteria for making ethical judgments, for one cannot act consistently over a period of time without guiding principles by which to make decisions. Also the church has an obligation to prepare its members to make an articulate Christian witness in their roles as citizens, workers, and members of families. Some members need more intensive instruction than others, for they are called to share in the actual work of teaching in the church school and other educational agencies. To some extent, however, all who belong to the church share in the responsibility of the church as a teaching community.

CONCLUSION

Biblically oriented and biblically grounded as they were, the early Baptists were in general accord with the New Testament understanding of the church. In the following chapter, we shall look at the way in which Baptists tried to develop a polity which would give outward form suitable to the inner being of the church. We shall then be better able to understand and to evaluate the validity and relevance of the Baptist witness.

III

The Church and the Churches

From the biblical view of the church, we turn our attention to specifically Baptist thought on this subject. Is Baptist ecclesiology in harmony with biblical teaching about the church? Do our formulations of doctrine parallel the vision of the church as seen in the light of God's intentions for it? Does our polity and practice faithfully express this concept of the church in visible forms? Such questions are crucial, since the historic emphases of Baptists revolve around them.

1. THE CHURCH IN IDEA AND IN HISTORY

Tensions between the Church and the Churches

By this time the reader will have asked himself, "What is the relationship between the church as depicted in the previous chapter and the actual churches with which we are acquainted? How is the *church* related to the *churches?*"

The church, as God intends it to be, is one and universal. In one of our favorite hymns we acknowledge this oneness as we sing:

Elect from every nation, yet one o'er all the earth;
Her charter of salvation, one Lord, one faith, one birth.

Actually, there is nothing more apparent than the fact that outwardly we are not one, but many. Herein is the first of three embarrassing contrasts. Instead of one catholic, or universal, church, we see a multitude of local congregations. Sometimes these are independent and unrelated to each other; sometimes they are connected along national, linguistic, class, racial, or confessional lines. Denominations and congregations compete with each other; and, within particular churches, factions strive for pre-eminence. On the surface it is difficult to recognize either the unity or the catholicity of the church.

Equally obvious is the contrast between the membership of the true church of Jesus Christ and the membership of the churches with which we are familiar. Surely, the church—as God knows it—is made up only of those who have been captivated by his Spirit. Yet within the membership of our churches are people who readily acknowledge that they are not committed Christians. Even those who are most dedicated show many marks of human sinfulness. Frequently our churches give the impression that they think of themselves as religious clubs, with overtones of a fraternal order or civic organization. Meeting with congenial people of their own kind, the members often reflect the social cleavages of the surrounding society instead of transcending such barriers.

A third contrast is found in the source of power. The church as a community derives its power from the Holy Spirit, whereas our churches often have depended upon institutional structures of power. In our eagerness to promote the work of the church we devise methods which frequently obscure the leading of the Spirit. Forgetful of our calling, we allow buildings, budgets, and programs to become ends in themselves.

One can sympathize with Dr. J. H. Oldham, when he remarks: "Christianity has no meaning for me whatsoever apart from the church, but I sometimes feel as though the church as it actually exists is the source of all my doubts and difficulties." [1] Although it is easy to bring such an indictment, we must remember that God works in and through the churches despite all the inevitable weaknesses of human material.

[1] J. H. Oldham, *Life Is Commitment,* page 79. New York: Association Press, 1959.

A Problem of the Reformers

These contrasts all point to the need for a definition of
the relationship between the church as it is in God's purpose
and the actual churches in which wheat and tares are mingled.
This question is what Prof. Emil Brunner has called "the un-
solved problem of the Reformation." How are the many separate churches related to the one church? How can earthly
churches with defects and imperfections be the church which
is the instrument of God's purpose? We cannot treat the
church and the churches as though they are completely identical, for the contrasts are too great. On the other hand, it is
not possible to separate them completely, for then we rob the
institutional churches of all significance. To state this question
in a pointed and practical way, we may ask, "How can the
church of Jesus Christ be expressed in such a way as to manifest its unity, catholicity, and holiness?" All Protestants including the Baptists have addressed themselves to this question, and
*it is in their answer to it that Baptists have made their pri-
mary contribution.*

Like the other leading reformers, John Calvin faced this difficulty. Appealing to the distinction between the "visible
church" and the "invisible church," he worked out an answer
to the relationship between the two. Since the latter is made
up only of the elect, and God alone knows who they are, he
concluded that we have no way of knowing who its members
are. Inasmuch, then, as the boundaries of the true church are
invisible to us, there is little point in trying to draw those
boundaries by a precise definition of membership. There is
no reason, therefore, why everyone should not be required to
belong to the outward churches. In that way everyone would
be exposed to the means of grace, including the discipline of
the church. Such a line of argument led to the continuation
of the parish-type church, in which everyone within a given
geographical area was included in its membership. Everyone
was enrolled by baptism as an infant. With a somewhat similar rationale, all the major Reformation churches justified their

practice of infant baptism. Baptists have traditionally rejected this viewpoint.

Although such terms as "visible" and "invisible" may have some convenience in discussing the church, they are misleading. It seems to suggest that the church has no visible existence on earth. This concept is not true, however, for in the church are real people who are "knit together in love through faith," and they share a common life. Their life in fellowship is created and sustained by the presence and power of the Holy Spirit. As a company of men who have been forgiven and who also forgive and forbear others, as a fellowship in which Christ lives and works, they are a redemptive community where the grace of God is mediated to men. It is merely the *limits* of the church that are considered as "invisible."

2. THE BAPTIST DOCTRINE OF THE CHURCH

The most distinctive emphasis of the Baptists was their threefold solution to the problem of the relationship of the church to the churches:

(1) They believed that the latter should reproduce, as nearly as possible in this imperfect world, the life of faith, obedience, and fellowship which characterizes the former. To this end, they rejected infant baptism, insisting upon believers' baptism.

(2) Holding firmly to the primacy of the universal church, they also insisted that each individual church represented the larger church in its locality, and had all necessary powers of self-government.

(3) At the same time, they devised ways to express the interdependence of local churches, so that the tendency to an isolated self-sufficiency would be avoided. Around these three points the Baptist doctrine of the church revolved.

Regenerate Membership and Believers' Baptism

Basic to all of their thought was a stress upon a regenerate church membership. They did not presume to play the role of

God, realizing that he alone knows with exactitude who are Christians and who are not. They did believe, however, that an approximate judgment could be made regarding those who belonged in a Christian fellowship. At least they were confident that no one who could not relate a convincing profession of faith should be admitted to the visible churches. In this respect they were at one with Congregationalist theory, but Congregationalists retreated from the full logic of their position by including the children of regenerate believers within the membership of a church. It was on this basis that Congregationalists retained the practice of infant baptism. Baptists, however, rejected this practice as inconsistent with the conviction that visible churches should strive to approximate the invisible church in the quality of its life. Nothing less than individual conversion would do as a qualification for membership; and baptism, they insisted, should therefore be restricted to those who "by a judgment of charity" were believed to be regenerate. As a guard against subsequent defection, moreover, a continuing discipline was to be exercised within the churches.

These Baptists were not perfectionists. They did not pretend that the boundaries of the visible churches correspond exactly with the invisible boundaries of the true church. Errors of judgment were not uncommon. Nor did they pretend that even the saints were free from human sinfulness. They were quite aware that imperfection taints everything human, even when the greatest care is exercised. "The purest churches under heaven," they said, "are subject to mixture and error."[2] What they did attempt to do was to restrict the membership to committed Christians, to those who made an open profession of faith in Jesus Christ as Lord and Savior. This was what they understood when they sought to achieve a regenerate church membership—not a sinless community, but a committed community.

[2] The Assembly or Second London Confession of Faith. W. L. Lumpkin, *Baptist Confessions of Faith*, page 285. Valley Forge: The Judson Press, 1959.

The Universal Church and the Local Churches

Besides the regenerate church membership, there is another main strand of the Baptist doctrine of the church. This is the attempt to magnify the importance of the local church without losing sight of the primacy of the universal church. The Presbyterian wing of Puritan dissent had emphasized the universal church to the neglect of the particular churches, while the Congregationalist party in New England had so stressed the place of local churches that they tended to obscure the view of the universal church.

The General Baptists

For the most part, it appears, agreement prevailed among General and Particular Baptists on these major issues regarding the doctrine of the church. If one reads the confessions of faith put forth by the early Baptists, he will be impressed by their clear convictions on these matters. It is instructive to read the following excerpt from "The Orthodox Creed" published by the General Baptists in 1678:

There is one holy, catholic church, consisting of, or made up of the whole number of the elect that have been, are, or shall be gathered, in one body under Christ, the only head thereof. . . .

Nevertheless, we believe the visible church of Christ on earth is made up of several distinct congregations, which make up that one catholic church, or mystical body of Christ. And the marks by which she is known to be the true spouse of Christ, are these, viz. Where the word of God is rightly preached and the sacraments truly administered, according to Christ's institution, and the practice of the primitive church; having discipline and government duly executed, by ministers or pastors of God's appointing, and the church's election, that is a true constituted church; to which church, and not elsewhere, all persons that seek for eternal life should gladly join themselves. And altho' there may be many errors in such a visible church, or congregations, they being not infallible, yet those errors being not fundamental, and the church in the major, or governing part, being not guilty, she is not thereby unchurched; nevertheless she ought to detect those errors, and to reform, according to

God's holy word, and from such visible church, or congregations, no man ought, by any pretence whatever, schismatically to separate. [3]

From the foregoing quotation it can be seen that these Baptists stressed the importance of the local church, while maintaining a proper appreciation of the universal church. The particular congregation was a focal point of the life of the church; it represented the church in a particular place. They were convinced that the fellowship of the Spirit is apt to be experienced most deeply in the smaller close-knit group. In the face-to-face relationships of the particular congregation, they saw a possibility of developing a corporate life where the Spirit can work more freely than in looser associations of people. Because the opportunity for members to know one another intimately is of such importance to the life of the church, an early confession states: "And therefore a church ought not to consist of such a multitude as cannot have particular knowledge one of another." [4]

To give visible expression to the universal character of the church, the General Baptists formed associational bodies in which delegates of the churches could meet. Such a representative assembly could also be called a church: "Churches appearing there by their representatives, make but one church, and have lawful right and suffrage in this general meeting, or assembly, to act in the name of Christ." [5] Thus the power of the local congregation to act as a church is balanced by a recognition of the interdependence of the churches and of the right of assembled delegates of several churches to act as a church in the name of Christ.

The Particular Baptists

In spite of the fact that the General Baptists and Particular Baptists differed in some matters of theology and practice, their basic doctrine of the church was practically identical. A

[3] *Ibid.*, pages 318-319.
[4] *Ibid.*, page 121.
[5] *Ibid.*, page 327.

reading of the confessional statements of the Particular Baptists reveals the same concern to preserve a judicious balance between the universal church and the local churches. Certain powers inhered in the local body, and these were jealously protected from encroachment by larger associations, but each congregation was to act responsibly in its relationships with others. As it was put in the earliest of the Particular Baptist confessions of faith in 1644: "Although the particular congregations be distinct and several bodies, every one a compact and knit city in itself, yet are they all to walk by one and the same rule, and by all means convenient to have the counsel and help one of another in all needful affairs of the church, as members of one body in the common faith under Christ their only head."[6]

A similar point of view is echoed in the confession of faith generally accepted by the majority of the Particular Baptist churches in England and in America. Known as the London Baptist Confession in England, it was called the Philadelphia Baptist Confession in America. Of great interest is the fact that the Baptists were so desirous of showing their affinity with other Dissenters that they adopted the Westminster Confession of Faith as a basis for their own statement. Quoting the Westminster Confession verbatim, page after page, they made significant modifications only in the articles which dealt with the church, the ministry, baptism, and the relationship of the state to the church. Not only does this document help us to see the close relationship which existed between Baptists and other Protestants, but it shows again the points at which they were conscious of their differences. The divergencies are centered in believers' baptism and church polity.

This confessional statement affirms a belief in the "catholic or universal church." With respect to the internal work of the Spirit, the Philadelphia Baptist Confession states that the church may be called invisible. It becomes visible to us, however, to the extent that it is made up of visible saints gathered

[6] *Ibid.*, pages 168-169.

in individual congregations. "To each of these churches thus gathered," it continues, Christ has given "all that power and authority which is in any way needful, for their carrying on that order in worship and discipline which he hath instituted for them to observe." [7] While each church has power to order its own affairs, it is not to live in isolation: "The churches . . . ought to hold communion amongst themselves for their peace, increase of love, and mutual edification. In cases of difficulties or differences, either in point of doctrine or administration . . . it is according to the mind of Christ that many churches, holding communion together, do by their messengers meet to consider, and give their advice in or about that matter in difference, to be reported to all the churches concerned."[8] The associated churches, to be sure, could not "impose their determinations on the churches," for the assembly of delegates did not have "church power." Nevertheless, a church was expected to heed the advice of the association or else be subject to exclusion from its fellowship.

The doctrinal statements of both General and Particular Baptists sum up the Baptist solution to the problem of the church and the churches. By requiring a public profession of faith and repentance prior to baptism and reception into the fellowship of a church, they sought to make the visible churches approximate the membership of the invisible communion of saints. In reply to the question of where the church may be seen here on earth, they said that it becomes most visible in a local congregation of professed believers. Each individual congregation was considered as a local expression, or outcropping, of the universal church, and each had power to govern its own affairs in consultation with others under the leadership of Christ its head.

In asserting that the church becomes most visible in local congregations, Baptists did not deny that it is also visible in larger bodies. The General Baptists specifically affirmed that

[7] *Ibid.*, pages 286-287.
[8] *Ibid.*, page 289.

the assembly of representatives of local churches should also be regarded as a church. The Particular Baptists made much the same point in their Discipline of 1798, by implication treating the association as another visible representation of the church. It is true that they denied that such a meeting of delegates had "church power," but that denial meant that this large body had no coercive powers to impose its will upon the local church. They were emphatic, however, in declaring the obligation of churches to join in a wider fellowship in which they should seek and accept the counsel of others. Moreover, both the statements (in their confessions) and their actions indicate that they did not limit their fellowship to others of their own denomination, but acknowledged themselves to belong to the catholic, or universal, church, which transcends all denominational lines.

A Baptist Definition of the Church

A useful and concise modern definition of the church is the one formulated by the British Baptists in 1926, which is as follows:

We believe in the Catholic Church [9] as the holy society of believers in our Lord Jesus Christ, which He founded, of which He is the only Head, and in which He dwells by His Spirit, so that though made up of many communions, organized in various modes, and scattered throughout the world, it is yet one in Him.

We believe that this holy society is truly to be found wherever companies of believers unite as churches on the ground of a confession of personal faith. Every local community thus constituted is regarded by us as both enabled and responsible for self-government through His indwelling Spirit who supplies wisdom, love, and power, and who, as we believe, leads these communities to associate freely in wider organizations for fellowship and the propagation of the Gospel.[10]

[9] The reference, of course, is not to the Roman Catholic Church, but to the total fellowship of all Christian believers everywhere.

[10] Ernest A. Payne, *The Fellowship of Believers*, page 143. London: Carey Kingsgate Press, 1952.

Such a statement is a faithful reflection of historic Baptist views. It takes account of the larger church as well as the local congregations where that church is embodied. It indicates the freedom of local churches in their responsibility to Christ, but also the inter-relatedness of congregations to each other. Without the use of terms which restrict the definition of the church to Baptists, or to a small segment of the church, it succeeds in making clear both the inclusiveness of the church and the Baptist interpretation of the visible churches.

3. HISTORIC DOCTRINES IN TODAY'S WORLD

We may now again ask the question with which we began: Is the Baptist concept of the nature and purpose of the church faithful to the New Testament understanding of the church? In the light of the foregoing survey of historic Baptist ideas, we may readily reply that the Baptist concept of the church accords with that of the Scriptures.

There remains, however, a corollary question. Is this concept also adequate to today's shifting sociological demands? Can it meet the practical requirements of the modern world? Its adequacy has been questioned at two points: (1) Is it possible to retain a consistent emphasis upon a regenerate membership? And (2) does Baptist theory provide satisfactory foundations upon which to develop an organization that is able to meet the challenge of a mobile and dispersed society?

Maintaining a witness to regenerate church membership has always been difficult. It must be acknowledged that our present practice is not consistent with our theory. Many influences have brought about a relaxation of standards for admission to church membership and permitted church members to treat their responsibilities lightly. If we were to take seriously the idea of regenerate churches, we would not ordinarily baptize children who are too young to make responsible decisions. The acceptance of persons into the fellowship of the churches would also involve a commitment to participate fully in the life of the church, and some form of discipline would need to be reinstituted. Although churches under these circumstances would be smaller, their witness would be more persuasive because of the committed, informed, and disciplined membership. Baptists have basic decisions to make. The temptation to be "successful" is strong, of course, and we may feel with Luther and Calvin that it is impossible to insist upon regenerate church membership. On the other hand, statistical success ought not to be our criterion. If we are convinced that our faithfulness to God requires us to be true to the basic features of our Baptist heritage, then we must make a renewed effort to make the membership of our visible churches approximate that of the invisible church which is truly the Body of Christ.

With regard to denominational organization, there can be no doubt but that our loose structural relationships have hindered our effectiveness. But is such a weak kind of organization necessary? Although the idea has somehow grown up that our particular structure of church government is scriptural, the fact is that it is supported neither by the Bible nor by historical Baptist ideas about the church.

As we have seen, the original Baptists tried to maintain a balance between the universal church and the local churches. Their successors have not been able to keep this balance, but have often stressed the local congregation to the near exclusion of the larger church. In nineteenth-century America, Baptists developed an exaggerated view of the autonomy of the local church, disregarding the strong sense of interdependence which had characterized earlier Baptist doctrine. It is that individualistic theory which underlies our present structure. A change of outlook is needed. Both the Bible and our historic principles require a more close-knit representative system of church government.

CONCLUSIONS

Therefore, the emphases which distinguished the Baptists at the outset of their history represented valid insights into the scriptural doctrine of the church. Until we are convinced that they are not biblical, we have a responsibility to keep them alive. It is not by abandoning our special emphases, but by reasserting and implementing them, that we shall foster the growth of stronger churches. To preserve regenerate churches, undergirded by believers' baptism and discipline, and to develop a better organizational pattern, are the challenges to us as Christians and as Baptists. Through the development of stronger churches we shall best represent the church of Jesus Christ.

IV

The Local Church

In order to fulfill its responsibilities under God, the church must be embodied in some visible shape in the world. Organizational structure is indispensable for expressing the life of the church and for the fulfillment of its purpose. No community can retain its character and achieve its aims without established patterns of operation. Therefore, orderly procedures must be adopted, and leaders must be designated and their functions defined.

1. THE QUESTION OF POLITY

In this chapter, attention will be devoted to questions having to do with polity, insofar as they affect a local church. What type of polity is most appropriate? By what criteria can such a question be settled? What are the processes by which the local church carries on its affairs? How is a church given a good start?

No Precise Pattern for Church Organization

It is commonplace for biblical scholars to observe that no single pattern of church government is prescribed in the New Testament. Christ laid down no detailed instructions for its outward organization, nor is any uniform organization re-

47

flected in the New Testament documents. In this respect, life under the New Covenant differs greatly from the minute prescriptions by which the life of Israel was ordered under the Old Covenant. The absence of precise regulations, however, does not mean that questions of church order are matters of indifference. "There are two opposite errors on this subject against which we must guard," declared Henry G. Weston in his *Constitution and Polity of the New Testament Church.* "The first is, that there is no church polity obligatory on Christians; the second, that everything in church life is so ordained in the New Testament that in every church, everywhere, and in all time, minute particulars must be identical." [1] Various alternative systems of church polity are allowable, but the variety of possibilities is not unlimited. Some of these are less appropriate than others, and, in fact, some are not in keeping with the character of the church at all. Wise and informed judgment is essential at this point.

Criteria for Determining Polity

Since the New Testament does not prescribe church polity, how does one determine what institutional forms are best suited to the use of the church? On the one hand, its structure will inevitably be affected by a desire for efficiency and by needs and conditions of society. Since the church is to serve the world, external factors must influence the activities, methods, and organization of the churches. It is evident that the early Christian communities adapted their organizational life to meet existing conditions. On the other hand, patterns and procedures of church life cannot be decided solely on the basis of administrative convenience or of accommodation to the needs of society. The nature and purpose of the church must always be kept clearly in view. The outward ordering of the life of the church must always be consonant with its vocation as a community which has been called by Christ and endeavors to live under his direction. The ultimate appeal in all questions

[1] Page 47. Philadelphia: American Baptist Publication Society, 1895.

of church order, therefore, must always be to what we know of Christ.[2]

2. THE FORM OF A LOCAL CHURCH

There is a mistaken notion that any "two or three" gathered together in Christ's name constitute a church. Christ, to be sure, may be present in the midst of any "two or three" gathered in his name, but such a company is not necessarily a church. To be a church, the London, Philadelphia, and Charleston confessions inform us, a community in Christ must be prepared "to walk

[2] The conventional approach to questions of church polity has been to distinguish three classical types of church government—episcopal, synodical, and congregational. The discussion then centers upon the respective claims of these three types of church government to represent the New Testament or apostolic church. Unfortunately this approach tends to obscure rather than clarify the issues, because these three types are frequently mixed, embracing elements of each. An apostolic episcopate as a separate and distinct ministerial or priestly order in the church, for example, raises quite different problems from the notion of an historic episcopate as a mere administrative office. A better approach to this whole question, therefore, is to identify specific opposing contentions and then to adjudicate their respective claims on the basis of their consonance with the community's understanding of the fundamental doctrines of the Christian faith.

Two key issues may be used to illustrate the method by which the claim to be a New Testament church may be tested. The first issue is posed by the "sacerdotal" conception of the church, with the clergy possessing unique powers as a separate and distinct order in the church. This conception was rejected by the Protestant Reformers as unbiblical, because it constituted a basic contradiction to the doctrine of the priesthood of all believers and denied to the individual believer full and responsible participation in the life of the church. The second issue is posed by the conception of a parish church embracing all the people in a given geographical area as over against the conception of a gathered church composed only of those who have made some profession of faith in Christ. The first view has been rejected by Baptists among others, because it fails to take into account the distinction between the old and new Israels. The continuity of the church with the old Israel, it is insisted, should never be permitted to obscure the fact that the basis of its life was radically altered when God sought to fulfill his ancient intention through a New Covenant in Christ with the people he had chosen and called forth. No longer was one to be incorporated into the body of his people by a natural birth but rather through faith in Christ. The new Israel was in the world but not of the world—a smaller society in the midst of the larger society in which its members were to live out their lives.

together before him in all the ways of obedience which he prescribeth" and must so order its common life that it may act responsibly in his name. What, then, are some of the basic considerations which determine the form of a church?

The outward ordering of the life of a church must, first of all, *make it apparent that it is a company of Christian people and not an indiscriminate multitude.* It is for this reason that a particular church has traditionally been defined among Baptists in their major historic confessions of faith as a company of faithful people, separated from the world by the Word and Spirit of God and having been baptized upon their own confession of faith, who consent or covenant "to walk together according to the appointment of Christ, giving up themselves to the Lord and one to another by the will of God in professed subjection to the ordinances of the gospel."

A community in Christ to be a church must, in the second place, *possess the means of grace appointed by Christ for ministering himself to the world.* A truly constituted church, all Baptist confessions have affirmed, is one which makes provision for the Word of God to be rightly preached, for baptism and the Lord's Supper to be truly administered, and for discipline to be duly executed.

In the third place, a truly constituted church must *be an ordered fellowship with officers of God's appointment and the church's election, and with specific procedures for determining God's will by the inquiry of the whole congregation.* Administrative provisions are necessary in any community, if only to avoid confusion and disorder. In a church it is also necessary to ensure that each member of the community participates as fully as possible, and that God's guidance be truly sought.

In the fourth place, a church must always *be aware that its very existence is bound up with its mission.* God has not called the church to enjoy privileges of security and comfort, but to a vocation of service to the world. It is not to be served, but to be a servant-people. Therefore, its organization must include the means of equipping the members for their ministry.

Through its common worship and its educational program, a church must enable its members to bear an effective witness as the representatives of Christ in every aspect of their lives.

Lastly, a truly constituted church *cannot exist in isolation from other churches.* It is but one particular manifestation of the whole church of Christ, and it must seek to maintain fellowship with other churches. Baptists have insisted that churches must hold communion with one another—meeting together through their representatives—for mutual edification, increasing love, preserving peace, bearing witness to their common unity, and whatever may tend to the furtherance of the gospel and the interest of Christ. And since, as they put it in their early confessions, "the purest churches under heaven are subject to mixture and error," each must seek the counsel and admonition of many other churches meeting together for the correction of its own life, so that it may act more responsibly in ministering Christ to the world.

3. THE POWERS OF A CHURCH

Baptists have always maintained that Christ has given local churches "all that power and authority which is in any way needful for their carrying on that order in worship and discipline which he hath instituted for them to observe." This was also the teaching of the Protestant Reformers. Martin Luther, for example, declared that it was incredible to suppose that "a little group of pious Christian laymen" who had been "taken captive and set down in a wilderness" could not constitute themselves a church and choose one of their number to preach and administer baptism and the Lord's Supper. Luther was insisting that the basic constituent element of a church is a faithful people and not any outward institutional succession. He was also insisting that, since all the faithful are priests, they may designate the person who is to act on their behalf as pastor. If these two contentions are true, there is no need for a company of Christian people to derive spiritual authority from any other source than Christ himself. But the last qualifying phrase makes it clear that no church is a law unto itself!

A church is subject to Christ. Congregational polity insists that all members must be permitted to assume the responsibilities of their mutual priesthood. That is to say, each member participates not only in the worship and work of the church, but also in the making of decisions which affect the common life of all the church members. Therefore, in a sense the church may be called a democracy, and it must utilize democratic or representative procedures. But it is a democracy only in a qualified sense, for Christ is the head of the church, and the members are his subjects. He is the king and the lawgiver, and the duty of the members is to render obedience to him. Thus, a church is really a monarchy: nothing should be allowed to infringe upon the crown rights of the Redeemer.

Judicial and Executive Powers

The basic powers of a church are judicial and executive rather than legislative. Since Christ is the lawgiver, as Baptists have often reiterated, the church has no legislative powers with regard to the fundamental considerations that determine its life. Its role is to discern the mind of Christ in both spiritual and temporal matters and to be obedient to him. Thus the powers of the church are judicial and interpretive on the one hand, and executive on the other, analogous to the responsibilities of a court to determine what the law is and that of executive agencies of government to apply it.

When Baptists, therefore, advocated a congregational form of church government, they did not do so because it offered a convenient administrative procedure by which decisions could be reached easily by a show of hands. They did so because they believed that Christ intended the full participation of the members of the church in its total life, as implied in the doctrine of the priesthood of believers. They also believed that, through such full participation, a church could be "a sensitive and delicate instrument" for searching out the will of

God. It was not that they considered congregational decisions infallible in their declarations of God's intentions. They believed rather that the full participation of all would provide a check to the distortion occasioned by self-regard, human limitations of knowledge, and vested interests.

Area of Permissible Legislation

Although it is undeniably true that a local church can have no legislative powers that supersede the fundamental teachings of the gospel or the inferences for church order derived therefrom, many other matters are of no particular theological significance. Changing circumstances often necessitate modifications of administrative arrangements that once were adapted to the needs of the church. Certain aspects of church life were once dictated by limitations of travel, but it does not follow that the church must always be geared to a horse-and-buggy era. Care must be exercised lest changes be introduced which distort or do violence to the understanding of the faith which they are designed to express. Whether corporate worship be in the morning or in the evening is a matter of relative indifference which may well be determined in the light of sociological considerations or the preference of the congregation. But even though the precise pattern of worship is not detailed in the New Testament, the content and structure of the church's worship cannot be decided with equal freedom. In similar fashion, although the New Testament does not prescribe the specifications for the building in which public worship takes place, architectural forms may have theological significance. Often the faith of the church becomes obscured quite inadvertently by incidental practices adopted without adequate reflection.

4. THE CHURCH MEETINGS

Among the Baptists, therefore, the church (or congregational) meeting has occupied a place of great importance. It has been the means by which God's will has been humbly sought and Christ's rule acknowledged. While certain executive responsibilities are assigned to the pastor, deacons, and other officers, the church has insisted that the entire membership is responsible to discuss, debate, and decide matters of basic concern to the life of the church. The church could not delegate its fundamental powers to boards or committees, nor permit them to be usurped by such boards or committees. The boards and committees could bring in recommendations, but decisions on policy matters belong to the church.

One distressing feature of contemporary church life has been the decay of the church meeting. There are several reasons for this decline, among which is the delegation of powers to small groups or individuals through simple default of members who are unwilling to accept their responsibilities. Even more responsible for the decay of the church meeting has been a mistaken understanding of the matters to be brought before it. Too often it has concerned itself with minor details of institutional life. Questions of spiritual, moral, and social significance in the life of the church and its members have been left to private reflection and decision rather than being brought under corporate consideration.

The Proper Concerns of the Church Meeting

In many cases the church meeting is preoccupied with the details of institutional housekeeping—with matters of finance and building maintenance, with the calendaring of events and the programming of activities. The general use of the term "business meeting" is a symptom of the restricted conception of its purpose. The planning of a Christmas party and the selection of a menu for a church dinner can safely be delegated, and it would seem equally obvious that the details of property maintenance need not demand the attention of the church meeting. The adoption of the budget falls within its necessary competence, but financial operations within the limits of budgetary provisions should be left to the designated officers. It is largely because such matters have been allowed to absorb the attention of the church meeting that its importance has been obscured, and interest in it has dwindled.

The proper concerns of the church meeting may roughly be divided into two categories: (1) the relating of worship to the internal life of the church, and (2) the relating of worship to the concerns of the members in their day-to-day life in the world.

With regard to the internal life of the church, the church meeting finds its focus in terms of the church's vocation. This involves a continuing discussion of the theological issues implicit in the church's confession. As issues are clarified, the church meeting must spell out their implications for all facets of the church's life. What these implications are for the reception, nurture, oversight, and dismissal of members must be carefully considered. Programs of evangelism must be reviewed to make certain they do not inadvertently distort or misinterpret the witness of the church. The relationship of children to the church must be determined, and careful attention must be given to the content of the instruction they receive. The structure of the services of public worship must be examined so that they may have both theological integrity and clarity of meaning.

Of equal concern to the church meeting are the issues confronted by the members in their daily life. The worship of God is the service of God, and it is not restricted to cultic acts. The church moves out into the world in the lives of its members, and God is worshiped through their obedience to him in their day-to-day activities and decisions. Because few of the issues they face—whether in the home, the office, the factory, the voting booth, or the legislative assembly—are transparently clear in terms of Christian duty, the members often desperately need the guidance and support of the corporate conscience of the church. It is within the context of the discussions of the church meeting that the implications of a Christian's obedience are clarified and a corporate conscience on specific issues is formed.

The Essential Features of a Church Meeting

The purpose of the church meeting is not to reach agreement among people of differing points of view. Its objective is not a sharing of personal opinions and individual preferences in order to reach a decision acceptable to all. The church meeting represents an earnest endeavor to ascertain the mind of Christ and thus the will of God for his people. To this end, there are several essential prerequisites to a properly constituted church meeting.

First of all, the church meeting presupposes *a prepared people*. It is not an indiscriminate gathering; it is an assembly of those who have made a profession of faith, have given some evidence of the sincerity of their profession, and have become members of the church. Nor should those who compose the meeting be merely nominal church members. If they are to participate in determining the affairs and witness of the church, they must avail themselves of the ordinary means of grace by attending the stated services of the church. They must allow themselves to be instructed by the preaching of the Word and to be nourished and strengthened by the fellowship of the Lord's Table. The mind of Christ is scarcely to be known by those who habitually neglect the disciplines which he appointed for his followers.

In the second place, the church meeting presupposes *a humble waiting upon the leading of the Spirit*. The guidance of the Spirit is invoked through prayer; the Scriptures are searched to discern whether or not the apparent guidance of the Spirit is truly of Christ; and attention is given to the voice of the church in the past as it has sought to understand and interpret the Scriptures.

In the third place, the church meeting presupposes *full participation* by the members of the church. It is the inquiry of the whole congregation as to the mind of Christ with regard to a specific issue. If only a minority of the membership is involved in making decisions, the congregational theory and its values are being denied in practice.

Since a congregational polity presupposes the full participation of members, and since a large congregation makes such involvement difficult, it is natural to ask whether the size of churches should be limited. How large can a church be and still be a church? The typical Baptist church today is larger than it was fifty years ago, its membership is more scattered, and work schedules of members are not uniform. To the difficulties of finding a time when all can meet is added the fact that effective deliberation becomes almost impossible when several hundred people meet together. We are confronted with the possibility that churches will become loose-knit associations of people whose sense of fellowship and involvement are minimal and who are poorly informed Christians.

Should churches be smaller? A realistic view of the situation does not allow room for expecting such a change, for a small church is usually handicapped by inadequate facilities, insufficient leadership, and a curtailed program. On the other hand, it must be noted that size alone does not determine such matters, for there are small churches where members do not participate fully and there are fairly large ones which find ways to overcome the handicaps of bigness. There is undoubtedly a point at which a church can gain nothing in effectiveness by increasing its size, and it should then give birth to another church. That point will differ with each situation, however, and each congregation must seek the mind of Christ as it relates to their own situation.

More important than an attempt to govern the size of churches is an emphasis upon making our larger churches more vital. Circumstances require that new means be devised for involving the whole membership in other ways than by the single, town-meeting type of assembly. In a situation where the entire congregation cannot meet at one time, there could be a modification of the church-meeting plan. Smaller groups can provide the experience of fellowship and the opportunity for thorough discussion of pertinent issues by which an informed and disciplined membership is developed. Good channels of communication can be established by which these smaller groups are kept related to the entire church. After such groups have considered matters of common concern, a larger representative church meeting may be better prepared to seek further light on such questions. Since the authority to arrive at decisions in policy matters and on significant issues should be kept in the hands of the congregation, an effort should be made to get as many members as possible to participate in the final, all-church stage of such church meetings. If the spirit and values of the congregational system are to be preserved, we must find ways such as these to foster Christian fellowship, to involve individual members in worship, study, and decisions of the church, and to prepare members to make informed Christian judgments in personal and social issues.

Lastly, the church meeting should be characterized by a *readiness to listen* on the part of its members. Each member, by virtue of his common priesthood, has the right to be heard, but he must also be prepared to listen, to learn, and to be instructed. Waiting on the guidance of the Spirit often means listening to others, for it is through them that the Spirit may speak.

Time and Frequency of Church Meetings

Except for the annual meeting, some churches have become accustomed to hold church meetings only intermittently and then only to settle a routine matter in the life of the church. This is unfortunate, for a church can have no common life—indeed, can scarcely be a church—unless church meetings are held with regularity and at frequent intervals.

Past experience would indicate that a monthly church meeting is most desirable, and it has most commonly been held on a week night. A basic requirement is that ample time be provided for the meeting so that discussion need not be hurried and the temptation to reach hasty decisions may be avoided. Some churches have found that a church dinner preceding the church meeting has the twofold value of providing added time and of creating a family atmosphere as a context for the meeting. Other churches have been experimenting with a return to an older pattern by having a dinner at the church once a month following the Sunday morning worship, and then holding the church meeting in the afternoon. This procedure has two distinct advantages. It places the church meeting within the context of the common worship of the church, and it provides an opportunity for the pastor in the sermon to provide instruction with reference to the questions to be discussed in the church meeting. The church meeting may deal with a particular theological point that needs to be clarified in terms of the witness of the church; it may consider the church's missionary obligation in some specific fashion; it may discuss some moral issue facing the community in order to provide guidance for the members. But whatever the subject to be considered by the church meeting, it is highly desirable that the discussion should be informed by whatever light the pastor can bring to bear upon it from his understanding of God's Word to his people.

5. RULES OF ORDER FOR THE CHURCH MEETING

In a congregational polity the vitality of a church depends to a large extent upon the church meeting. Therefore, Baptists in the past were careful to define certain procedures necessary to a properly constituted church meeting. The intention was to make it as clear as possible that the entire congregation was engaged in seeking the mind of Christ.

1. *There must be a competent moderator.* In the past, Baptists almost always have held that the pastor should be the moderator. They spoke of his "presidential authority," by which they meant his right to preside at all meetings of the church. Occasionally, it was regarded as wise that someone else serve in such a capacity, but only in exceptional circumstances.

The reason for such a requirement was that it seemed necessarily related to the pastoral office. The pastor had been chosen to be the leader of God's people in a particular church, the shepherd of the flock; and to permit someone else to preside might obscure the pastoral image. Furthermore, the pastor was the expert interpreter of the Scriptures, and as chairman he could give the competent theological guidance needed in the determination of affairs.

Today, many feel that it is more appropriate to select someone else from the congregation to preside at such meetings. The arguments to support such an arrangement are twofold. In the first place, such service enables laymen to be more involved in the life of the church. These responsibilities can be assumed by someone who has gifts of leadership, but does not have the specialized training which would make him an authority in theological matters. Thereby the pastor is freed from some of the administrative chores which interfere with his other duties. Also he is actually free to take a more active part in the meeting than if he were the chairman. Ordinarily the presiding officer does not have liberty to participate in the discussions, and thus the pastor who does not preside can make a larger contribution to the meeting. In the role of a resource person, he can give a kind of leadership which is better adapted than that of moderator to developing an informed and working church.

Individual churches, therefore, will do well to weigh the foregoing arguments for and against the pastor's serving as moderator, and make a decision based on their own local situation.

2. *An orderly procedure should be followed.* The meeting should be opened with a prayer invoking God's presence and the guidance of his Spirit in all deliberations. The minutes of the previous meeting should be read and approved. Routine business should be quickly dispatched so that a discussion of such matters is not unduly prolonged. The major matters to be considered by the meeting should then be clearly stated, so that there may be a proper division of time allotted to each. The meeting should be closed with prayer, asking God's blessing upon the decisions that have been reached.

3. *All must be heard.* The church meeting is an inquiry by the entire church and the possibility must always be kept in mind that the Spirit may speak through the humblest of the brethren. The more articulate and self-assertive should not be allowed to monopolize the discussion to the exclusion of others. Each person, therefore, must be given full opportunity to speak, and the words of each person should be carefully pondered.

4. *Unanimity should be sought.* The principle of unanimity has been important in congregational theory, for the church is not a political organization which can be satisfied with a mere majority vote. The objective of the church meeting is not to win a vote, but rather to discern the mind of Christ. When a decision is not concurred in by the whole church, the mind of Christ has evidently not been made clear. Such a decision would have dubious spiritual authority. The difficulty of involving a large number of people in a deliberative process leads to the temptation to delegate all important decisions to small committees or boards. In matters of basic policy which affect the church as a whole, however, every effort should be made to find time to reach a clear consensus before a decision is made.

5. *Dividing the church should be avoided.* A primary obligation resting upon the church is to "maintain unity in the bond of peace." If a mere majority decision cannot be made unanimous, it is usually preferable to delay the decision, rather than run the risk of dividing the church. Occasionally a church may feel that it must make a decision before it reaches a common mind and before it can win unanimous consent, but under such circumstances no action should be taken which cannot command at least a two-thirds affirmative vote. Even then the action can be taken only with grave misgivings and regret. Furthermore, if such action threatens seriously to divide the church, then the decision should be postponed until the counsel and advice of the association or state convention has been obtained.

6. Counsel and advice should be sought. It has been the custom of Baptists when confronted by perplexities to address inquiries to the association or state convention in order to secure counsel and advice. In response to such inquiries, either the matter is discussed and the requested advice given, or a committee is appointed to counsel with the church. Usually the inquiries represent merely a desire for further light concerning matters in which the church is able to discover no clear guidance. In such situations, the seeking of counsel and advice is purely permissive. But in those situations which threaten to divide the church, no action should be taken until counsel and advice has been sought and an opportunity has been provided for representatives of the association or state convention to endeavor to effect a reconciliation between the two opposing factions.

6. PROCEDURE FOR ORGANIZING A CHURCH

The right to form themselves into a church resides in any company of Christians, and this is a right which cannot be abrogated without restricting God's own freedom to call forth a faithful and obedient people. Baptists traditionally have thought of churches as coming into being in three stages. The intention to be a church must be present, and this intention finds formal expression in a covenant with God and with one another. This constitutes a church *essential.* When a constitution for the orderly government of the church has been adopted and officers have been chosen, they become a church *completed.* Then, having petitioned the Baptist association in the area for admission and having been welcomed into its membership, they become a church *recognized.*

Such a local church comes into existence in a variety of ways. Sometimes a convention or associational missionary gathers the group that is to be formed into a church; sometimes a church emerges from a mission outpost of another local church; sometimes an individual Christian will take the initiative. Although those to be formed into a church may be gathered in different ways, there is an orderly procedure which should be followed by Baptists in the actual formation of a church.

1. The counsel and advice of the association or the state convention should be sought at the outset, and a request should be made to either of these two bodies that a person, preferably a neighboring minister, be appointed to serve as convener and moderator of their meetings.

2. The sponsorship of a neighboring church, willing to dismiss a group of its members to form a nucleus of trained leadership for the proposed church, should be sought.

3. Those who propose to organize the new church should then, under the leadership of the appointed moderator, be formed into a *conference,* so that they may meet together in orderly fashion in advance of the actual organization of the church. They shall seek to ascertain their common understanding of the Christian faith and of the nature and mission of the church, and they shall proceed to the consideration of a proposed church covenant and constitution. During this period, the members of the conference should meet together for common worship and should make interim provision for a Sunday school.

4. The proposed covenant and constitution should be submitted to the association or state convention for counsel and advice, and the services of a lawyer should be secured to make certain that there will be full compliance with the requirements of state laws relating to religious corporations.

5. Arrangements should then be made to baptize those new converts who purpose to become members of the new church, and to secure letters of dismission from other churches for those proposed members who are entitled to such letters. A committee should be appointed to examine, with the assistance of the person appointed to act as convener or moderator, both the letters and the candidates. These procedures will normally take several months.

6. When preparations have been carefully made, all who purpose to become members of the new church should be in-

vited to attend a meeting specially convened for the purpose of its formation. After prayer invoking God's presence, the covenant previously agreed upon shall be read and accepted by a show of hands. Those accepting it shall then proceed to sign their names to it, thus forming a church *essential*. The moderator shall then ask the guidance of the Holy Spirit in their further deliberations. A constitution for the orderly government of the church shall then be adopted, and the officers of the church—including a pastor and deacons—shall be elected, thus constituting a church *completed*. The meeting shall be closed with prayers invoking God's blessing upon the church.

7. The newly constituted church shall then petition the local Baptist association for admission into its membership. Upon favorable action by the association, the church becomes a church recognized, in full and regular standing. It is desirable that there shall be a service of recognition, at which the church shall be formally welcomed into the fellowship of the association.

The local church, then, is the visible expression of the church of Christ in a given locality. Acknowledging Jesus Christ as its head, it defines its powers and procedures in keeping with this relationship to Christ. Crucial to its life is a continuing attempt to seek the mind of the Lord of the church, and Baptists have believed that the entire congregation is responsible to engage in this process. Therefore, the church meeting should be the local church's primary instrument, for when it ceases to function effectively, the health of the church is affected. Essential to vital congregations are committed members and capable leadership. We turn, in the following chapters, to discuss the qualifications of church members and qualifications and duties of the various church officers.

ADDENDUM

SPECIAL PROVISIONS RELATING TO CHURCH MEETINGS
RECOMMENDED FOR INCLUSION IN CHURCH CONSTITUTIONS

Notice of Intended Action. The laws of most states provide that certain matters cannot be decided by a church meeting without previous notice having been given of the intention to act upon such matters. This restriction most frequently applies to the calling or dismissing of a pastor, the buying or selling of real property, and the incurring of a legal indebtedness. The most common provision is that notice of such intended action shall be given from the pulpit on each of the two Sundays immediately preceding the meeting at which the action is to be taken. If the laws of a particular state do not impose such a restriction, it would still be wise for the church to incorporate it in its own constitution.

Denominational affiliation. Since some churches have been taken out of their denomination either by minority groups at sparsely attended church meetings or by virtue of misinformation used to mislead the members, churches have found it highly desirable to include some such provision as this in their constitutions:

This church shall adhere to and be a member of the American Baptist Convention, the _____ Baptist State Convention, and the _____ Baptist Association, and shall not resign or withdraw from any of these bodies except by a duly adopted amendment to the Constitution of this church upon petition for such resignation or withdrawal signed by two-thirds of all the members of this church; nor shall such action be taken until at least thirty days have elapsed following a consultation thereto by the Boards of Deacons and Trustees of this church with the Moderator of the Association and the President of the State Convention or their representatives.

Notice to the State Convention prior to the calling of a pastor. Churches not infrequently have called men to be their pastors, much to their later regret, on the basis of insufficient information. Unfortunately, there are men who have displayed weaknesses of character, personality, or ability, who have found their way into the ministry. In order to guard against a call being extended on the basis of insufficient information and to avoid being misled by an outwardly prepossessing personality, some churches have thought it wise to include some such provision as the following in their constitutions:

This church shall not call a minister until thirty days after the pulpit committee has requested the office of the _____ Baptist State Convention to supply information concerning the record and qualifications of the candidate it proposes to recommend to the church.

The thirty-day provision would seem to represent the minimum time required by the state convention office to make inquiries and to assemble information concerning the list of possible candidates submitted by the pulpit committee of the church. This provision should not delay the calling of a pastor, for usually it will take at least two weeks to settle on a particular candidate and to arrange an interview, and ordinarily two more weeks elapse before a vote can be taken extending a call. Nor does the provision in any way infringe upon the freedom of the church to call whom it will.

Amendments to the constitution of the church. Since the church was recognized and welcomed into fellowship by its Baptist association on the basis of the constitution which it had adopted, it would seem to be common courtesy to notify the association of any proposed changes in the constitution. Furthermore, the experience of other churches may suggest problems and difficulties that would be created by the proposed change which had not occurred to the members of the particular church. For these two reasons, it may be desirable to include the following provision in the constitution:

> This Constitution may be amended only after thirty days have elapsed following notification to the Moderator of the _____ _____ Baptist Association of the proposed amendment or amendments.

V

Church Membership:
Qualifications and Responsibilities

BAPTISTS EMPHASIZE THAT THE MEMBERSHIP OF VISIBLE CHURCHES should include only those persons who are sincere Christians. But they have also been ready to acknowledge that an infallible judgment of a person's relationship to God is impossible. For this reason various Baptist confessions conceded that even "the purest churches under heaven are subject to mixture and error."

It is not necessary to conclude that if we cannot do something perfectly we should not try to do it at all. We need not give up all efforts to determine who are fit material for church membership. To do so would be to surrender the claim that Christ has laid upon us and to give up all endeavor to express the true life of the church in any visible, tangible way. Although one's profession of faith cannot be tested in any ultimate sense, that fact does not mean that a profession of faith should not be required of those who wish to enter the fellowship of the church. Anyone who has yielded his life to God in Christ should be able to state simply what it means to him to be a Christian, and his life should give some evidence of the sincerity of his profession of faith. Thus an individual is baptized only after he has made a public profession of faith

67

and has been examined by the church. In this way, and by explicit provision for subsequent nurture and discipline within the fellowship of the church, Baptists have tried to realize the ideal of fully committed churches composed only of believers.

1. ADMISSION TO CHURCH MEMBERSHIP

Ways of Receiving Members

Baptist churches receive members in three ways. First, new members are received *by baptism,* after having made a profession of faith. Second, persons coming from another church may present a letter of commendation, and be admitted then *by letter.* Third, there are some people who have once manifested faith in Christ and been baptized, but through carelessness their contact with the church was not maintained and their relationship with God grew cold. When such a person repents of the lapse which has occurred, he should not be rebaptized, nor can he be certified by his former church as a member in good standing. He is received after making a statement of his Christian experience, expressing repentance and an intention to dedicate his life anew to Christ. This practice is called receiving people *upon experience,* because its basis is their statement of previous Christian experience. Sometimes a fourth category of admission is used, namely, *by restoration.* This indicates that a member is received back into fellowship after having been excluded from the church. Such a case, however, is not essentially different from one who is accepted upon experience and need not be treated as a distinct classification.

Preparation for Membership

Baptist churches of previous centuries used to require those wishing to join a church to appear before a congregational meeting to give a testimony to their experience of God's grace. Although not everyone had had a dramatic conversion, each person was expected to have made a decisive commitment and to tell simply what it meant to him to accept Christ as Savior and Lord. When he had declared his faith, an opportunity was presented for the pastor and others to ask questions to clarify points about which they wished further information. The candidate was then asked to withdraw, so that the congregation could discuss the question of his admission. If his testimony had been convincing, the congregation voted to accept him into their fellowship. Care was taken not to arrogate to themselves the ability to discern perfectly the mind of God, but after careful deliberation the members made what they called "a judgment of charity."

Modern practice differs considerably from that of early Baptist churches. As congregations have become larger and their memberships more scattered, there has been a weakening of the bonds of fellowship. In many churches, particularly in the South, it is common to have a congregation vote upon the reception of a member immediately upon his signifying an intention of joining the church. A person may indicate his desire to unite with the church by coming to the front of the sanctuary at the close of a service, and the congregation will be asked to vote without further information than can be given at that time. In the Baptist churches of the North, it is more usual to have a person appear before a membership committee prior to a congregational vote.

If it is to act responsibly before God, a church must exercise all reasonable care to see that those who are received are fully committed to Christ. It is therefore imperative that those who ask to become members of the church receive instruction and be examined. A sincere profession of faith in Jesus Christ as Savior and Lord is the only real test of eligibility for church membership. The only theological knowledge which can be required of a new convert is an understanding of the rudiments of the gospel. In order to be as sure as possible that a candidate has these qualifications, a church must make provision for instructing each one in the meaning of church membership and for testing the genuineness of his profession of faith.

Discipleship classes for those seeking membership should be standard practice in all churches. Such training is necessary for both the young people and older persons who are entering upon the Christian life. Even those who come from some other denominational background need to be instructed about Baptist emphases. Indeed, the fact that people have been church members for years does not ensure their understanding of the essential elements of the gospel or of the meaning of church membership. Therefore, it is well to require all prospective new members to attend a discipleship class taught by the pastor before being received into the church.

The amount of time which should elapse between an initial profession of faith and baptism depends upon the background and maturity of the persons in question. Those coming directly out of a pagan environment, as is the case on some mission fields, are expected to go through a period of probation. During that time they receive further instruction, and their lives are observed by the church to see whether they are serious in their purpose to live as Christians. Some form of probationary period might well be reinstituted even in the older churches.

It is difficult to know at what age children should be admitted into church membership. Many Baptist churches today encourage the baptism of children of eight or nine, but it is doubtful that those who are so young are prepared to make the significant decision which is required. There was a time when Baptists seldom baptized people under sixteen, and usually those who came into their churches were older than that. There are exceptions to most rules, but the rule should probably be to expect youth to reach twelve or thirteen years of age, at least, before joining a church. One reason why we have so many nominal Christians today is our careless admission standards. To be so careless is tantamount to treating the faith itself with contempt, and to baptize children too early is virtually to return to a practice of infant baptism.

Examining Applicants for Membership

After instruction, *a candidate should be examined by the Board of Deacons*, acting as a membership committee. At that

...tify to the reality of his Christian
...on to engage actively in the life
...tality of his life to the lordship
...ked which would elicit from
...ating his understanding of the
...nd his intention to be loyal to Christ

...pproval of New Members

...Deacons are satisfied with the statements of the
...e, they recommend to the church that he be received
...member, following baptism or receipt of his church letter.
*...he entire congregation should approve or reject a candidate
in a regular church meeting.* Ordinarily, there should be
unanimous agreement before a new member is admitted. In
open meeting opportunity should be given for anyone to express his reasons for opposing the acceptance of a given individual. No one has a right to vote against a person without
good reasons which he is willing to communicate to the church.
So that the bond of fellowship will not be broken, there ought
to be unanimity among the members.

Soon after the church has signified its approval, a baptismal
service should be held, and baptism should be administered
to those who have not already been baptized. *The "hand of
fellowship"—the formal welcome of the person into the membership of the church—is then extended at the first communion
service after the baptism, although it may be done at some
other time if necessary.* The hand of fellowship is a brotherly
greeting to a new member, but it is not essential to membership.

2. MEMBERS' RESPONSIBILITIES AND PRIVILEGES

Church membership involves responsibilities, but that fact
unfortunately has not been always made clear to everyone.
By joining a church we become a party to a covenant in which
we acknowledge our relationship to God and to one another.

Church Covenants

During the seventeenth century, it was the nor
of Baptists to form a new congregation by covena
God and one another to walk together in all the ways
would make known to them. The persons who were to
stituent members of a church would draw up a covena
at a formal meeting would sign their names to the docu
The act of covenanting made explicit the vows implie
baptism, and their act was the means of constituting
church. New members consented to accept the terms of th
covenant, and periodically entire congregations renewed their
covenant vows. Although not uniformly adopted by all Baptists, the practice of forming a church by covenanting with
God and with one another was a common pattern in America.

The use of covenants in forming a church is reflected in a
seventeenth-century definition of a church. Benjamin Keach,
a Baptist minister of that period, described a church as "a congregation of godly Christians, who at a stated assembly (being
first baptized upon profession of faith) do by mutual agreement and consent give themselves up to the Lord, and one to
another, according to the will of God." Although the word
"covenant" is not used in this statement, the writer is describing the covenanting by which a visible church was constituted.

Although the language in which early covenants were
couched differed somewhat, the general outlines were much the
same. The essential idea was expressed as follows: "We do
hereby give ourselves up to the Lord and to one another,
agreeing to walk together in all of the ways which he does
make known to us." In some cases the covenant contained
little more than this simple statement; more often it mentioned
specific duties which a member accepted as binding upon him
as a member of a church.

It is not uncommon for Baptists to read a church covenant
today in connection with their observance of the Lord's Supper, but this usage is often little more than a formality. Few
people know the significance of the covenant idea in the history

of their churches, and little attempt is made to impress upon them the significance of their words when they read this document together. It used to be customary for Baptists to hold a covenant meeting on a weekday prior to the monthly observance of the Lord's Supper. At that time the church family gathered to testify to their religious experience and to renew their covenant with God and one another. The recovery of such a practice today could help to impress upon us the significance of our covenant obligations and prepare us for a more meaningful celebration of the Lord's Supper.

The use of such covenants is a most suitable means of impressing upon church members the sacred obligations which accompany their Christian profession. A church may draw up such a document for its own use, or it may adopt one prepared for general use in the churches. A covenant should include only things which inhere in the Christian life. Trifling things and customs based upon peculiar cultural conditions ought not to be included in its obligations. The covenant which is most common among Baptists today is an adaptation of earlier ones, particularly of one which was framed in connection with the New Hampshire Confession of Faith. A more modern one also appears in the Appendix (p. 209).

In one paragraph, that covenant affirms a responsibility to co-operate in the work of the church. Beginning with the words, "We engage . . . to strive for the advancement of this church," it enumerates ways in which its life will be supported. When one becomes a church member, it should be clearly understood that he is going to participate actively in its life. It is a travesty upon the nature of the church when members attend worship services irregularly and exhibit no interest in its work.

The Responsibilities of a Church Member

In a large church the program is often so complex that no individual can be involved in every activity. However, everyone can and should participate as fully as possible in the worship, educational ministry, and business of the church. As a minimum he should attend worship services weekly, unless hindered by illness or absence from the vicinity. He should also be enrolled in some program of systematic study. When there is evidence that a person is indifferent to such responsibilities, it becomes the business of the congregation to inquire into his motives. Those who are negligent toward their duties should be reminded of them. There is no more justification for having inactive members of a church than for having inactive soldiers in an army.

Members are responsible for serving in the church program when given the opportunity to do so. Those who have ability to teach, to hold office, or to perform some other task, should gladly devote the time and energy necessary to do the job thoroughly. There are varieties of gifts, and there are many kinds of service, all of which contribute to the smooth operation of the whole body.

Everyone is obligated to contribute generously to the financial support of the church. Stewardship involves not only the investment of our personal talents, but the use of our material possessions. What is liberal giving for one person will not be so for another, and a comparatively small contribution may represent a really sacrificial offering for a person of limited means. The New Testament does not lay down a rule requiring that everyone give a tenth of his income to the work of the church, but that is a good proportion for an average family to try to give. Most people give more than that amount involuntarily to the government in taxes; and by cutting down on some of our spending for things which are not necessary we can do that much for the work of God. A person who is grudging in giving to the cause of Christ evidences a spirit that runs counter to the love of God and of one's neighbor which Christ has enjoined upon us.

Besides an interest in the work of the local church, Christians are concerned for the co-operative work of churches of their own denomination and that of interdenominational agencies.

It is a temptation to be so preoccupied with immediate interests that our outlook becomes provincial. While the local congregation is the focal point of the life of the church, there must be ways in which the larger church of Christ presents its witness and shares common tasks.

In another section of the usual covenant we "engage to watch over one another in brotherly love," thus acknowledging our duty toward those who are of the household of faith. Having been assured by their testimony that they are Christians, and having accepted them into the fellowship of the church following baptism, we receive them as Christian brothers and sisters. Our kinship is through a common participation in Christ; and our love is based upon higher considerations than the ties of blood or the sharing of common background and interests. Within the Christian community we have our opportunity to express most fully that love by which Christ said that men should recognize his disciples. It is the mark which sets the church apart as a demonstration of that new society which God is creating and of which the church is the nucleus.

Love toward Christian brethren is expressed in many ways. Among other specific things mentioned under this heading are these: "to remember each other in prayer; to aid each other in sickness and distress; to cultivate Christian sympathy in feeling and courtesy in speech; to be slow to take offense, but always ready for reconciliation, and mindful of the rules of our Savior, to secure it without delay."

To pray for each other is an obligation and a privilege of church members. Our interest in our brethren should be expressed in intercessory prayer, as we seek God's blessing upon his people. For those in need of material things, for those who are bereaved or lonely, and for those who through weakness have lapsed into sins, we must offer our prayers to God. For the corporate witness of the church, for the work of our congregation in its community, and for the pastor and other leaders of the church, we lift up our hearts and voices to God.

When prayer represents a sense of responsible concern, it will be accompanied by efforts to minister to the needs of others. Hence, there must be a willingness to bear burdens, and to share joys and sorrows. Today, when government has had to assume responsibility for assistance to the needy at so many points, there is a tendency to lose all sense of personal interest and responsibility for aiding others. Although we should rejoice that such relief is made available to those in need, we should not lose all personal interest in them. Most churches can have some share in ministering to families and individuals within their own ranks, who are faced with hardships. Where the possibilities of giving financial aid end, there is still a place for sympathetic understanding and a ministry of Christian friendliness.

Furthermore, members are duty-bound to promote the unity and harmony of the church. Wherever human beings associate closely, tensions and conflicts arise, but in the church every effort should be made to resolve the conflicts and remove the tensions. Although truth and right are not to be disregarded, there should be a willingness to forbear and forgive, and a ready acceptance of persons in spite of their shortcomings. Made up of men who have known God's pardon, the church is to be a community where forgiveness and sympathetic understanding are readily offered.

As individuals in every family must often subordinate their own desires to the interests of the group, so within the church self-interest must be curbed. Here is the place to express best that love which does not envy and is not arrogant or conceited. Although we are familiar with churches where there is party strife and where unhappy divisions have occurred, such a spirit is a denial of the meaning of Christian brotherhood and should be shunned. Even though we who compose the church are subject to human limitations, a power is available through the presence of Christ which enables us in some measure to overcome our human tendencies toward pride and selfishness.

Moreover, in the covenant we pledge ourselves to use aids available for the cultivation of our spiritual and moral development. While Christianity is not to be confused with moralism, it nevertheless involves a way of living and has a concern for ethical conduct. We do not seek to merit God's approval by our achievements, but in gratitude for God's goodness and mercy we seek to obey him. This obedience includes the development of integrity, courage, concern, love, purity, and faith.

Membership in the church should inevitably make us open to God's leading. Thus, we try to ascertain how our Christian vocation may be fulfilled in all of the relationships and roles of life. If we are to learn God's will in these matters, and to have the resources of faith and courage to act accordingly, we need to increase our understanding of the Scriptures, to share in the worship and discipline of the church, and to maintain a private devotional life. Honest self-examination and humble confession of sins are necessary to growth in Christian life, and these are to be followed by the endeavor to alter our lives for the better at points of acknowledged weakness.

Finally, membership in the church implies willingness to bear witness to Christ. The ministry belongs to the church as a whole, and every member has a duty to share in that ministry in his own way. The New Testament makes no distinction between ministers and laymen, for all are ministers and all are of the laity.[1] There is, however, a difference between "pastor" and "laymen," for the former term signifies one who is chosen by the church to occupy a position of leadership. Hence, we all share in the ministry of the church, but we do it in different ways.

[1] *Laos* is the Greek word from which we get "laity" and "laymen." It means "people," and all members are included among the "people of God." In our common parlance, we use the term "laymen" to distinguish specialists from those who do not have special training in a particular field. In that sense, it is proper to speak of laymen in the church, meaning thereby those who do not have the special training for exercising the pastoral leadership. Nevertheless, the term tends to be misleading.

Every Christian represents the church in the world; in fact, the church member may be thought of as being at work on the frontiers between the church and the world. He makes his testimony clear by what he does, says, and is, whether on the job, at home or in the community. Through the church he should receive insight and strength to live as a Christian in his vocation, not simply through verbal means but through attitudes and relationships. Accepting responsibility for the nurture of his own children, he seeks to provide the kind of environment in the family which will encourage them to become Christians. This kind of witness is something which occupies every day of the week, and involves all of life.

The Privileges of a Church Member

Church membership involves privileges as well as duties. There are certain rights which accompany membership in a Christian church. A member has a right to participate in the whole range of the church's activities—its worship, witness, service, and business affairs. As one who has a part in governing the church, a member has a right to be heard and to vote on any issue under consideration. Full opportunity should be afforded for all who wish to declare themselves on matters relevant to the life and faith of the church. If time does not permit all to be heard at a particular meeting, another occasion should be appointed when they can express their views. It must be remembered that God does not automatically speak through majorities, and he may speak through a minority of one. So long as a person speaks and acts in good faith, he has a right to a hearing.

3. THE TERMINATION OF MEMBERSHIP

Having discussed the admission of members into a church, we need also to consider the ways in which members are dismissed. There are *three main methods* by which dismission is effected—*by letter of commendation, by erasure,* and *by exclusion.* The most common means is the transfer of membership from one congregation to another by letter. When a person moves from one community to another, he should present himself for membership in a church near enough to his residence for him to participate regularly in its life. The church to which he thus applies should request a *church letter* from the one where he is a member. Such a letter indicates that he is in good standing, and that he is being dismissed from their fellowship to that of the new church. If the person in question is not in good standing, the church letter should provide that information. When a church has received the letter, it should acknowledge receipt of it.

It is the practice of some churches to grant letters of dismission to individuals, so that they may present them at some future time to a church where they may move. However, many times such letters are retained by individuals for a period of years, because the person does not affiliate with any church. These people have been called "trunk Baptists," because their letters are packed away in their luggage. Such procedures are not very satisfactory. After the passage of months or years, these persons can hardly be said to be members in good standing of the church to which they formerly belonged. Any church to which they presented themselves ought to raise serious questions as to their reasons for neglecting to identify themselves with a church for a prolonged period of time. It is better to grant letters of commendation only upon the direct request of a church. Then persons who move away and break their ties at home and remain unaffiliated will have to be received into membership on some other basis. The receiving church would then have an opportunity to impress upon them the responsibilities of church membership before accepting them into its number.

Partly because admissions practices have been lax, every church of any size has members on its rolls who cannot be accounted for and others whose attendance is very infrequent. In some churches two rolls are kept, one for resident and the other for non-resident members. Some may leave all of the names on a single roll, while others periodically remove the names of persons who take no active part in the work and worship of the church. The removal of names of persons who cannot be accounted for is called *erasure*.

The third way in which membership is terminated is *exclusion* from the fellowship because of scandalous behavior, teachings which embarrass the cause of Christ, or failure to live up to covenant obligations. Baptists used to call this "excommunication"; today that term has been dropped from the vocabulary in favor of the word "exclusion." However, whatever term is used, the fact is that the practice which it represents has virtually disappeared from our churches.

Although such a radical kind of surgery should be taken only after great patience and care have been exercised, there are times when persons should be excluded from the fellowship. Since the church is meant to be a living embodiment of God's people, the Body of Christ visible in this world, those who are habitually indifferent ought not to be on its membership list. Careful efforts should be made to enlist the active participation of delinquent members. It is much better to win people back to loyalty to Christ and his church than to drop them from membership. However, after such efforts have been made to no avail, they should be excluded from the church. The term *inactive members* is a contradiction in terms when applied to the church. When a member dies, his name is erased from the church roll, and there is no more reason to retain those whose indifference reflects spiritual deadness than to keep on it the names of the deceased.

4. THE QUESTION OF OPEN MEMBERSHIP

By the middle of the twentieth century, new problems arose concerning the dismission and reception of members. According to traditional Baptist practice, letters were always granted only to churches of "like faith and order," and only those persons who had been immersed on a profession of faith were admitted as members. Baptists were convinced that their doctrine of a regenerate church membership could not be maintained if members were transferred by letter to and from pedobaptist denominations. To receive members from pedo-baptist churches by means of letter, they held, was tantamount to giving approval to infant baptism; and infant baptism seemed clearly incompatible with the conception of a regenerate membership. For generations, therefore, Baptists adhered to their historic stand. Like the Episcopalians, they stated that letters were granted only to churches of like faith and order. When a letter to a church outside the Baptist family was requested, they responded by writing that the person in question was a member in good standing, and that his name would be erased if the other church were to accept him on a statement of Christian experience.

Changing conditions, however, brought a challenge to Baptist practice. The mobility of families and the growing consciousness of a need for Christian unity led many congregations to re-examine their policy regarding the admission of pedobaptists. As it became more common for families to change denominational affiliations when they moved to new communities, there were more frequent requests for Baptist churches to grant letters to, and to accept letters from, other denominations. The problem was especially acute in growing metropolitan areas where, by comity agreement, a Baptist church might be the only Protestant church in a neighborhood. A pervasive ecumenical spirit had also made people more aware of the essential oneness of the church of Jesus Christ.

In the face of this situation, an increasing number of Baptist churches have adopted an open-membership policy. That is, they admit persons from pedobaptist communions without requiring them to be rebaptized subsequent to their profession of faith. They expect the applicant to give evidence of a sincere profession of faith in Jesus Christ and of having been baptized and confirmed in his former church. On the other hand, most Baptists have resisted such changes and consider them a betrayal of Baptist principles. A standing resolution of the American Baptist Convention (May 26, 1926), which stated that "only immersed members will be recognized as delegates to the Convention," has been rescinded.

The Case Against Open Membership

Probably the great majority of Baptist churches today still insist upon believers' baptism by immersion as a requirement for membership. They defend their position by an appeal to the Scriptures, to Baptist history, and to practical considerations. On these grounds they offer a strong case for continuing to insist upon believers' baptism by immersion as a requirement for membership in Baptist churches.

Approaching the question of baptism from the standpoint of the Scriptures, they insist that the rite must be associated with a decisive experience of faith and repentance on the part of the one baptized. Only by going beyond the evidence, they say, can one make a case for baptizing a passive individual on the grounds of the faith of someone else. Moreover, the evidence strongly supports immersion as the mode of baptism practiced in the apostolic era. Therefore, on scriptural grounds alone they regard the question as settled. They go on to point out that, with only a few exceptions, Baptists through the years have regarded believers' baptism by immersion as the only acceptable form of the rite. Since this practice seemed inseparably connected with the ideal of a regenerate membership, Baptists in the past have insisted that the latter could be maintained only by retaining an emphasis upon believers' baptism.

Some have also bolstered the arguments from Scriptures and from Baptist history with pragmatic observations. Pointing to the experience of Protestant Europe, they argue that the scandalous situation there illustrates the inevitable outcome of practicing infant baptism over a long period of time. In several countries, the state churches claim memberships which comprise the majority of the citizens, but only a small minority takes any serious interest in the life of the churches. Indeed, many Protestants in Europe seem to have uneasy consciences with regard to infant baptism. Therefore, these Baptists declare, it would be foolish to abandon a position which has such strong biblical and historic support, and substitute one which has such demonstrable shortcomings.

The Case for Open Membership

There are other Baptists, however, who are not satisfied to uphold the traditional Baptist practice in this way. They contend that more problems are raised by refusing to admit pedobaptists to membership in Baptist churches than by admitting them. They, too, are concerned to be faithful to the witness of Scripture, but they explain that we are closest to the mind of Christ when we emphasize the spirit and purpose which underlie outward forms of ecclesiastical practice. In support of their stand in favor of open membership, they appeal to the essential meaning of baptism in the New Testament and to its significance for Baptists. By such consideration, these Baptists believe that it is possible to preserve the scriptural intent of the rite and the historic Baptist emphasis of believers' baptism without conforming to the outward form in all details.

Those who espouse this position agree that baptism should be related to the repentance and faith of the person who is to be baptized. Since they are advocating the reception by letter of persons baptized as infants, the question is raised: Can infant baptism have a connection with faith and repentance? Most other Protestant churches staunchly maintain that it can and does have such a meaning. The baptism of infants is tacitly acknowledged by many Protestants to be incomplete until the individual has accepted his baptism and made a public confession of faith. Vows of confirmation, or something corresponding to these, are regarded as the completion of a process begun at baptism. Only after confirmation is the person fully a member of the church and eligible to partake of the Lord's Supper. In a sense, it is held, the two acts become a single event, and baptism becomes associated with faith and repentance. The sequence of events is admittedly awkward, they say, but they add that this reversal and separation of the parts of baptism began fairly early in the history of the church and Christians today must make the best of the situation. Feeling that it is presumptuous to declare most Christians unbaptized, some Baptists are willing to admit therefore that infant baptism followed by confirmation constitutes a *broken but valid* form of baptism.

Secondly, turning to the question concerning the significance of baptism in relation to regenerate church membership, it is asked: Can regenerate membership be realized without strict adherence to the practice of believers' baptism? Admittedly, most of our Baptist forefathers would have returned an emphatic negative to that question. But early in our history, we are reminded, there were a few voices among Baptists which dissented from the prevailing opinion on this point. John Bunyan, for example, held that "the church of Christ hath no warrant to keep out of the communion the Christian that is discovered to be a visible saint." In examining this matter, it is stressed, one should clarify the issues and base his conclusions upon principles rather than upon expediency.

Contrary to the general assumption, argue those who favor open membership, believers' baptism is not an indispensable prerequisite to regenerate churches. Unless one is willing to contend that believers' baptism by immersion is essential to regeneration, they say, he cannot very well assert that regenerate church membership depends upon that form of baptism. No one questions that there are in pedobaptist churches many persons whose vital Christian experience and deep consecration leave no doubts that they are twice-born. The history of the church offers ample evidence that God has not withheld his Spirit from those who have been baptized as infants. Therefore, it seems necessary to concede that regenerate church membership is not inseparably tied to believers' baptism.

The quality of church membership, state the advocates of open membership, depends more upon the preparation and examination of those admitted into it than upon the kind of baptism which is administered. Baptist experience, they contend, demonstrates that churches of poor quality can result even when believers' baptism is retained, if inadequate attention is paid to examination, nurture, and discipline of members. An emphasis upon the quality of the Christian commitment of applicants, therefore, is more significant to them than the requirement of a particular form of baptism.

It is not the intention of those who hold such views to minimize the importance of baptism. Their purpose is to focus attention upon what they regard as primary, so that we shall not be diverted by a preoccupation with secondary things. It is neither believers' baptism nor infant baptism which is the decisive factor, they assert, but faith in Jesus Christ as Savior and Lord. According to their position, baptism is an external form which is intended to signify a deeper reality. While no command of Christ is to be dismissed as trivial, we must not mistake form for substance. In the matter of baptism as with other ceremonies, they say, one may be so careful about proper compliance with ritual requirements that the act is reduced to legalism. If such a reduction is to be avoided, they conclude, and if we are really interested in the ideal of regenerate membership, our emphasis must be upon the care with which we admit members and the subsequent nurture which is provided for them.

To support open membership, say those who favor it, is not to propose that Baptists abandon believers' baptism. In our own practice, they explain, we must adhere to believers' baptism by immersion. Although a broken form of baptism may be accepted for Christians from other churches when their lives testify to a genuine Christian commitment, there is no reason for Baptists to adopt such a form for their own usage. Baptists recognize the obvious incongruity in administering baptism prior to a profession of faith, and the difficulty of associating such a baptism with repentance and faith. Moreover, there is a vivid symbolism in immersion which is lacking in either sprinkling or pouring; immersion dramatically portrays one's identification with Christ in his death, burial, and resurrection. Therefore, from the standpoint of the New Testament, believers' baptism by immersion is the appropriate form, and it ought to be retained by Baptist churches.

Individual Churches Must Choose

With respect to the question of open membership, then, there seems to be no simple, neat solution of the problem. Although traditional Baptist practice which insists upon believers' baptism by immersion may seem to present the stronger case, there is also both logical and theological force in the open-membership position. Until the impasse can be broken, both viewpoints will continue to find expression in Baptist churches. Meanwhile Baptists need to seek further light under the guidance of the Holy Spirit, as they try to arrive again at a clear consensus on this issue.

Whichever position is adopted, it is necessary that the essential meaning of baptism be kept in mind. To continue to stress regenerate membership in local churches requires that we take care at the right places. Churches should seek to ascertain whether the baptism and confirmation of persons coming from other churches does represent a sincere commitment to Christ. The same careful scrutiny which is given to new converts should also be given to those who ask to be received by letter from another church. That care should be exercised whether the applicant comes from another Baptist church or from another denomination. No church should succumb to the temptation to make standards of membership easier simply in order to increase its size. Moreover, careful attention should be given to continued nurture and discipline of the member, encouraging his Christian growth and enlisting him in its ministry.

VI

The Baptist Ministry

A BASIC CONSIDERATION DETERMINING THE FORM OF A CHURCH is the possession of appropriate officers. Among Baptists a church *completed* was traditionally defined as one having officers of God's appointment and the church's election. "A particular church," states the Philadelphia Baptist Confession, "gathered and completely organized according to the mind of Christ, consists of officers and members; and the officers appointed by Christ to be chosen and set apart by the church . . . are bishops, or elders, and deacons." Having treated some aspects of the local church in the preceding chapters, we now turn to the subject of officers essential to a church.

1. OFFICERS OF A LOCAL CHURCH

The chief office bearer in Baptist churches of an earlier day was the pastor (also called elder or bishop), who was to preach, teach, counsel, admonish, and rule. Deacons were to assist the pastor by looking after temporal affairs of the church, so that the pastor's attention need not be diverted from his main responsibilities. In some cases, a Baptist church also elected a ruling elder to assist the pastor in governing the church, and in some there was a teaching elder to help with the educational aspect of the work. Neither of the two latter offices had any function independent of the pastoral duties, however, and they did not become permanent among Baptists. With a dearth of qualified persons to serve in such positions, and with small congregations making them unnecessary, they gradually disappeared.

The New Testament Churches

When Baptist leaders of an earlier century customarily spoke of the offices of pastor and deacon as being "appointed by Christ," they were voicing a conviction that these were the two divinely prescribed offices essential to a church. In principle, at least, Baptists were correct in this interpretation, although they did oversimplify the New Testament data. Since their time, biblical scholarship has demonstrated that the form of the ministry in the primitive churches was too varied to be reduced to a single pattern.

Instead of a picture of uniformity of church officers, the New Testament records reveal variety. They reflect a situation in which institutional patterns were being established but had not yet become fixed. Although no exact model is furnished for churches to follow in determining their officers, some principles are given for their guidance. Officers, like polity, must be considered in relation to the nature and purpose of the church. Certain offices are essential to the being of a church, while others vary with the needs of a given situation.

Perhaps one might expect to find more specific patterns of church offices in the New Testament, but examination of relevant passages will show that the writers gave little attention to such details. One cannot always distinguish between functions within the life of the church and specific office-bearers in its organization. For example, in his first letter to the Corinthians, Paul wrote: "And God has appointed in the church first apostles, second prophets, third teachers." He seemed to be enumerating the particular offices in the church, but his list continues: "then workers of miracles, then healers, helpers, administrators, speakers in various kinds of tongues" (1 Cor. 12:28). The latter categories refer to particular spiritual gifts and functions, but there is nothing in the statement to distinguish the first three terms from those which follow. It is also noticeable that no mention is made of pastors, bishops, elders, or evangelists in this list. Apparently the writer was thinking of spiritual gifts rather than offices in this context.

In Ephesians Paul wrote that Christ had given special ministerial gifts to his church: "And his gifts were that some should be apostles, some prophets, some evangelists, some pastors and teachers" (Eph. 4:11). It sounds as though these gifts are meant to be related to offices within the church. However, no further description of them is offered, and again we are left with questions as to his meaning. Are each of these terms intended to refer to distinct positions within the church? If so, were they to be temporary or permanent? Does the same person combine the work of pastor and teacher? If this is a list of church offices, why were not deacons included?

When the foregoing passages are compared with 1 Timothy, additional questions are introduced. In this letter there are definite references to particular offices. Nothing is said about evangelists, apostles, or prophets. In chapter 3, however, the qualifications of a bishop and of a deacon are stipulated. In the discussion of deacons, a reference is made to "the women," but there is uncertainty about its meaning. Are they deaconesses, or are they wives of deacons? Later, in chapter 5, there is a cryptic statement about "the widows," as though they may have occupied a special position in the church. Still farther along is the statement: "Let the elders who rule well be considered worthy of double honor, especially those who labor in preaching and teaching" (1 Tim. 5:17). Who is the elder? Is his a distinct office, or is this term synonymous with bishop and pastor? If the latter is the case, then why would only some of them labor in preaching and teaching? Elsewhere in the New Testament are references to a plurality of elders in a given congregation.

These allusions suggest that no uniform system of organization had been crystallized in the apostolic churches. The solution to the problems raised by the biblical data lies in recognizing the transitional character of this period. Only gradually did the Christian community see clearly that its identity was to become completely separated from Judaism. Consequently, it was slow in developing its own organizational forms; and when it did, it took over familiar patterns from the synagogue organization and adapted them to the new situation.

In the synagogue were boards of elders (presbyters), which served as governing bodies, and one of their number was the presiding officer ("the chief ruler of the synagogue"). As new Christian congregations were established, they appointed boards of elders to administer their affairs. Among the elders were individuals to whom special responsibilities were assigned, and perhaps some of them were called bishops (overseers). As the church was extended and the number of believers multiplied, there arose a need for a greater division of labor. Duties connected with worship and teaching were assigned to bishops (or pastors), and distinctions began to be made between bishops and other elders (or priests).[1] With the rise of new needs, new offices were apparently created, as in the selection of seven men for administering the distribution of the common fund (Acts 6:1-6). The choice of the seven has traditionally been considered the beginning of the diaconate, but this fact is far from clear. By the end of the second century, a threefold ministry of bishops, priests, and deacons had developed in several centers.

It is a mistake then to expect to find in the New Testament an organizational structure which can be literally copied today. If the practice of early churches, as disclosed in the biblical records, was so varied, we may assume that it is unnecessary for us to duplicate any one pattern that was used in the primitive churches. The church is an organism, and its outward form may vary. Within certain limits, its organization is flexible and adaptations may be made to meet changing conditions.

---

[1] The Greek word for elder was *presbyter,* and *priest* is a shortened form of *presbyter.*

Guiding Principles for Determining Church Offices

Nevertheless, the absence of exact forms to be followed does not imply that there are no guide lines. To agree that the pattern of organization developed in response to practical needs does not mean that it was a completely accidental or indiscriminate development. *The nature of the Christian community and its mission to the world supplied guiding principles which governed the development of specific offices.*

It may be useful at this point to take a backward look for a moment. In the second chapter, the church was portrayed as a people called by God to be the agency in and through which he is working out his redemptive purpose. As a nucleus of persons who had experienced the transforming power of God, they were to continue the ministry of Christ in the world. Restored to fellowship with God and brought into closer fellowship with other men, they were to be a redemptive community serving human need. The corporate nature of the Christian community is stressed in many figures of speech, and its ministry is shared by all its members.

The Priesthood of Believers

The characteristically Baptist belief that the ministry belongs to the church as a whole is expressed in the doctrine of the priesthood of all believers. Unfortunately, this doctrine has often been misunderstood, for its conventional interpretation is that it means no more than the right of every man to approach God directly. It is true that Christ is our High Priest, and that his priestly work is unique and unrepeatable. We may indeed come to God in prayer and in humble confession of our sins without the intercession of a human advocate, but for that matter people under the Old Covenant could also do that! This interpretation is not what the doctrine of the priesthood of believers was originally intended to stress; it emphasized responsibilities more than rights. The idea of priesthood indicates something done on behalf of another; one cannot be a priest to himself.

The conception of the priesthood of believers was formulated in the Reformation era, but its foundations are in the New Testament. While the idea is implicit elsewhere, one of the few places where it is explicated is 1 Peter 2:9, "But you are a chosen race, a royal priesthood, a holy nation, God's own people, that you may declare the wonderful deeds of him who called you out of darkness into his marvelous light." This statement, which was based on words originally addressed to Israel (Exodus 19:5-6), is applied herein to the church of Jesus Christ. The writer's obvious intent is to declare that as God's people, the church has a priestly ministry similar to that of Israel. The idea of the priesthood of believers, therefore, might be more clearly expressed as the mutual ministry of all believers.

It was with this idea in mind that Martin Luther announced that all members of the church are responsible ministers of Christ. Every man is a priest, and thus there is no special priestly class which has a monopoly on the means of grace. Nothing in the New Testament encourages the idea that a special clerical class was to be created which would be responsible for worship and witness, while the great majority of members would be spectators. Nevertheless, now as in Luther's time, there is a subtle tendency toward clericalism, which separates the status and functions of pastors and laymen in a misleading way. The employment of the term "full-time service" to designate those who work in specialized church vocations has fostered the impression that people are serving God only when they are engaged in some activity of the institutional church. The implication seems to be that the interests and occupations which take up the major part of the time of the average church member are unrelated to the service of God. In order to correct false impressions about such service, we need to broaden our conception of the church's ministry.

First of all, the limited idea that the church exists and serves only when people are gathered for some formalized church service needs to be dispelled. The church exists even when its members are dispersed in their homes and at their jobs, and its ministry is carried on through all of the roles and relationships of individual Christians. Not everyone bears his witness or carries out his Christian vocation in exactly the same way, but everyone is called to serve Christ in all of his life. As John Calvin put the matter "[God] has appointed to all their particular duties in different spheres of life. And . . . he has styled such spheres of life *vocations* or *callings*. Every individual's line of life, therefore, is . . . a post assigned him by the Lord."[2] Looked at in this light, it is plain that members serve God in a wide range of ways; and all of these are part of the church's ministry to the world in the name of Christ.

The Need for Leaders

With the thought very clearly established in our minds that the ministry belongs to the entire congregation, we may proceed to discuss the need for leadership within the churches. It is important to guard against clericalism's opposite extreme, which sees no need of leaders with professional training. We must remember that, although all members of the church are ministers, not all of them are pastors. The distinction is one of role or function. There are diverse kinds of ministry, and among them is a ministry of leadership in the church whereby the entire fellowship is trained for its responsibilities. According to Paul, Christ's gifts to his church were "for the equipment of the saints for the work of the ministry"[3] and "for building up the body of Christ" (Ephesians 4:12). Gifts of leadership are needed to help the whole church develop spiritual maturity so that it is prepared to fulfill the calling it has received from God.

It should be self-evident that churches need leaders in order

2 John Calvin, *Institutes,* III, x, vi, translated by John Allen. Philadelphia: Presbyterian Board of Publication.

3 Recent scholarship has indicated that the comma which follows the word "saints" in earlier versions, such as the King James and Revised Standard, should be omitted. See, for example, *The New English Bible* (Oxford University Press and Cambridge University Press, 1961).

to be faithful to their calling. This necessity is implied in Paul's enjoinder that things be done "decently and in order" (1 Corinthians 14:40), and it is involved in the concept of the church as analogous to the human body. Declaring that Christians have diverse gifts, Paul compares them to different parts of the body. It would not be good, he says, if the body were all eyes or ears; but each gift within the church supplements the other gifts, as varied parts contribute to the total functioning of a human life (Romans 12:4-5; 1 Corinthians 12:12-28). His point is obvious; namely, that all who make up the church contribute to the fulfillment of its task, each one according to the gifts that God has granted him.

The doctrine of the priesthood of all believers, therefore, does not eliminate the necessity for some division of labor within the church. In his discussion of this subject, Martin Luther said that it is possible, in theory, for everyone in town to be the mayor; but from a practical point of view, only one person at a time can hold such an office. Although many persons might be able to assume certain offices in the church, the requirement of doing things "decently and in order" necessitates that specific persons be designated to serve in particular positions. Leadership is needed to help a group focus its efforts and achieve its purposes with a minimum of waste and confusion. Even in the primitive churches, there were some specialized leadership functions which required the establishment of particular offices, and the expansion of Christianity brought about further differentiation of functions. The offices were associated with special responsibilities for leadership.

Those who serve in such offices act as representatives of the church. That is why Baptists insist that officers of a church be elected by the body. Since no one has a right to represent other people without their approval, a congregation must approve the officers who are to act in its behalf. It is this principle which underlies the ordination of men to specialized ministries, as well as the election, or call, of the pastor and other officers.

If a church is to act responsibly in the name of Christ, it needs some leaders with specialized training in the pastoral office. To this office special responsibilities are charged, and for its fulfillment special gifts and preparation are required. There are other kinds of ministry which require the dedication of able people, but which offer opportunities for leadership by those without professional training. The rest of this chapter is devoted to a discussion of the office of the pastor, and the succeeding one deals with other offices of the church.

2. THE PASTORAL OFFICE

What is the work of the pastoral ministry? In the past when life was more simple, the pastor's role was relatively clear. He was the leader of the congregation, the shepherd of the sheep (as the word "pastor" literally means), who was accountable to God for those who had been placed under his care. Nor did he need to inquire what his duties were. He led the public worship of God, presided at other meetings of the church, instructed the faithful from the pulpit, catechized the children, visited the homes of those who had made no Christian profession, baptized converts, counseled the perplexed and distraught, performed weddings, and conducted funerals. His schedule of activities was apt to be fairly simple, although by no means easy. Mornings were devoted to study so that he might properly instruct the people, afternoons were devoted to visitation, and evenings were spent with the family or at occasional church gatherings. Living within a convenient radius of the meeting house, the individual members of the church could be intimately known by the minister.

The pastor's role in the twentieth century is not so clear-cut. It has tended to be obscured by many new demands that have been placed upon him. Congregations are larger and more scattered. This circumstance has meant a loss of intimate personal relationships, a larger number of weddings and funerals, and a vastly increased need for visitation. The dispersed membership involves many hours spent in travel; in fact visits to two or three hospitals may pre-empt a whole afternoon. Not only are congregations larger and more scattered, but their organization has become more complex and cumbersome with a multiplicity of boards, committees, and special-interest groups. As a result, heavy promotional and administrative demands are placed upon the pastor, transforming him into an executive secretary whose principal business is to keep the organization functioning efficiently and smoothly. Far from being a leader of a people, he is often regarded as an employee who is skilled in looking after details. He is also expected to represent the church by participating in a wide variety of community activities and to attend the endless schedule of church meetings. Little time is left for study and reflection, and it becomes increasingly difficult for the pastor to know what is his primary vocation. Is it to be a leader of God's people, an interpreter of God's word to them, and a physician of souls; or is it to be an efficient administrator of ecclesiastical machinery, a recreational director, and a public relations man?

One of the most important tasks confronting the churches in the twentieth century is the task of restoring to the pastoral office its proper image.

The Role of the Pastor

What, then, is a pastor? In the light of our concept of the church as a worshiping, teaching, witnessing, ministering community, what ought the role of the pastor to be? What kind of leadership should he be expected to provide? The pastor's role is primarily an inside job. His task is to "equip the saints for the work of the ministry" and to "build up the body of Christ" (Ephesians 4:12). Through his leadership the church as a whole must come to an understanding of its own nature and mission, with its members learning how they themselves can be missionaries and evangelists living on the frontiers between the church and the world.

At the very heart of the pastor's work is his teaching ministry, which is a part of almost all that he does. Only as church members are informed and disciplined are they equipped to live in obedience to God and bear a faithful witness to him. The church regards the Scriptures as having a unique authority for faith and practice, and an understanding of the Bible is imperative for Christians. If Christians are to understand the Scriptures adequately, they need disciplined study under competent guidance. Without pastors who have special training in the Bible and in theology to instruct them, church members are open to the whims of self-appointed authorities who may introduce all sorts of vagaries. The Bible is not a book that can be easily understood. There is much that an untutored person can understand in the Bible, of course, and sometimes a man of simple faith has insights which are not given to a more learned man who does not have the same spirit of commitment. However, the plain fact is that the Bible can be a dangerous book when it is misunderstood and misused. It is only necessary to remember that many of the most bizarre and exotic cults claim to be based squarely on the Bible, to appreciate what happens when uninformed interpreters become authorized teachers.

The risk that individual interpreters without knowledge may fall into queer aberrations which falsify Christ is not the only one in Bible study. There is also the fact that the church lives in the world, and must constantly guard itself against the pressures of the world, which serve to distort the gospel. The conformity-making influence of culture is a constant threat. The history of Christianity is filled with examples in which the gospel has become identified falsely with some elements of a given culture. Such dangers are so subtle that only by a clear understanding of the Bible and by solid theological thinking can the church maintain its identity as a church of Christ. Without members who are solidly grounded in the Christian faith and its implications for the whole life, the church stands unguarded against the danger of being molded by the environment in ways that are inconsistent with its very nature.

The vocation of the pastor includes the conduct of public

worship of God. Not everyone has the gifts of training to conduct such a service in a manner conducive to a genuine encounter with God. Furthermore, there would be chaos if everyone arrogated to himself the responsibility to take the lead in such services. This does not mean that worship is limited to the times when the whole congregation is gathered together, nor that no one but a pastor can pray or read the Scriptures. Indeed, worship should also be at the heart of small-group activities, and teachers and officers should be able to lead such gatherings in devotional periods. The pastor, however, is authorized to assume leadership in the corporate worship of the church. This authority is delegated to him, not because he is endued with some special grace that others lack, but because good order demands that someone be chosen and because the congregation believes him to be qualified for it. In the same way, baptism and the Lord's Supper are acts of the church, which may not be performed in orderly fashion without the consent of the church. Such consent is expressed in ordination and a call to pastoral responsibility, and normally these acts may properly be performed only by an ordained pastor.

Equally prominent in the pastor's role is the duty of teaching. While many share in the instructional life of the church, the pastor is the chief teacher. He is a teacher of teachers and plays an important part in the preparation of leaders in all of the church offices. When a pastor is chosen, it is partly because he has exhibited gifts which make him a good teacher, and because he has been given specialized education in disciplines related to the life of the church. As a pastor he is freed for study so that he may be able to interpret the Scriptures, showing their relevance to the situation of his people. As a preacher and teacher, it is his peculiar responsibility to help the church understand the will of God with regard to contemporary needs and issues.

Another important aspect of the pastor's work is the care of individual souls. In a small church the pastor can have close ties with all the members and share in an intimate and personal way all their joys and sorrows. In a large church this is more difficult, but it is still important for the pastor to have a personal acquaintance with all of those to whom he is called to be a shepherd. Where he cannot establish the close and intimate relationships which prevail in a small membership, he can nevertheless help to develop patterns of church life which will enable people to experience the fellowship of the Holy Spirit. Much can be done toward such an end by developing smaller groups within which individuals will experience the kind of intimate fellowship which helps them to become mature and articulate Christians. Much of the pastor's time will be occupied with urgent personal problems which require his individual attention—the problems of people who are troubled by anxieties of one kind or another. Men, women, and children whose lives are shattered by homes that are broken or torn by strife and dissension are to be found everywhere. In every community there are parents whose children are in revolt or involved in delinquent behavior. Other people are troubled by a sense of alienation from God, by a feeling of personal inadequacy, by the drudgery and meaninglessness of their jobs, or by the fact that youth is slowly slipping from their grasp. All of these need the healing word which can be brought by a wise and well-prepared pastor. Even in this kind of ministry, however, the entire church should have a share, for troubled persons need the therapeutic effect of becoming part of a fellowship of Christian friends.

Although a pastor may become too much involved in administrative duties, a certain amount of such work is properly a part of his responsibility as a leader of the church. Others may do much to relieve him of routine administrative duties, so that he can give himself more fully to the tasks which alone are his. If he can prepare others in the church to assume administrative duties, he ought to delegate responsibilities to such people. The pastor, however, cannot abdicate responsibility for general oversight of the total program of the church.

The Qualifications of a Pastor

It is clear that the pastor must be equipped with the "gifts" of leadership, including an aptitude for study, balanced judgment, and an ability to communicate clearly and persuasively. His character, as the New Testament informs us, should be beyond reproach. In addition, he should have a profound concern for people and a sensitivity to their needs and unspoken yearnings. This kind of interest will spring from a deep experience of the reality of God's redeeming love in his own life. Clear convictions as to the essentials of the Christian faith are also necessary.

Although these "gifts" are basic, it goes without saying that careful preparation is also needed to equip persons fully for pastoral leadership. A winning personality and dynamic energy may be enough to get results of a sort, but more than personality and vigor are needed to build up the body of Christ. A broad knowledge of the world in which we live and an understanding of human needs are important for the pastor, and graduation from a liberal arts college is therefore considered essential to an adequate preparation for the ministry. But college training is not enough. A thorough familiarity with the Scriptures—the "source" book of the Christian community—is indispensable. There are right ways and wrong ways of using it, and the wrong use of the Bible may produce demonic results. Furthermore, the insights of the Bible must be brought together in a structured whole—into a systematic theology—if their meaning is to be made plain and their implications apprehended. Finally, because he needs to be able to communicate the gospel effectively, he must be familiar with the processes by which people learn, as well as with the hidden motivations which impel them to act and to behave as they do. Therefore, the theological education which a seminary offers is indispensable. When we speak of pastoral ministry as a learned profession, we mean that a pastor should be learned in the Christian faith and in the ways of the world, and that he should have those skills which will enable him to help people to develop a mature Christian faith. His education will not make him an adequate minister without the prior possession of "natural" and "spiritual" gifts, but neither will he be adequate without careful and disciplined preparation for his task.

The Call to the Ministry

The term "call to the ministry" is somewhat misleading, for, as has already been stated, all Christians are called to be ministers. What is meant by the term is the call to the pastoral ministry. Many people seem to think that a calling to such service is purely a private matter between an individual and God. Some people declare that no one has a right to question another person's sense of call to such a ministry, no matter how unsuited that person may appear to be. Such a completely individualistic interpretation of the call of God is not in line with Baptist thought prior to the middle of the nineteenth century. Since the pastor preaches and teaches and ministers in a representative capacity, the call of God is an outward call which comes through the church. The inward call or the secret call is an inner assurance on the part of the individual that it is God's will that he should make himself useful in the role to which the church has summoned him. Such an inward call finds expression in his willing response to the outward call of the church.

If the ministry belongs ultimately to the church itself, then it is the responsibility of the church to select worthy persons to act as its representatives in exercising leadership in the ministry of the whole church. The early Baptist churches were constantly being reminded to seek out those young men among their members whose "gifts" and aptitude for learning suggested that they might have the capacity for pastoral leadership. The initial call of the church to them might be a word spoken by a pastor, a deacon, a church school teacher, or some other member. If there was an answering response and a conviction by the whole church in the genuineness of the "gifts," the procedure was to license him to preach so that he might exhibit his "gifts" and to encourage him to pursue the necessary studies to equip him for pastoral labors. The final step was then for him to present himself to the church for ordination. Before he was ordained, his call, his Christian experience, his educational preparation, and his understanding of the Christian faith would be reviewed and examined by an ordination council, and a decision would be made as to his suitability for the pastoral ministry. Ordination, therefore, became a public affirmation by the church that an individual's qualifications had been tested and that he had been approved for the pastoral ministry.

In the twentieth century the role of the church is much less clear. Too often the church neglects its responsibility to take the initiative in suggesting to some person that he should consider whether or not God is calling him to the pastoral ministry. Indeed, it is not uncommon to have someone say to a young person: "If you can possibly do anything else, stay out of the ministry." While this advice is well meant, it is misleading, for it suggests that one must receive some sign utterly different from that of other callings if he is to be a pastor. Furthermore, it falsifies the role of the church, which again and again—as in the case of John Knox, for example—has had to labor and pray and almost compel men to assume the pastoral responsibilities for which God had so obviously equipped them.

Ordination to the Pastoral Ministry

According to the customary practice among Baptist churches, it is the local church that ordains a person for the pastoral ministry. A local church, however, should have the counsel and advice of other churches in so important a matter. Therefore, other churches of its local association are represented in the ordination council which examines the candidate and recommends to the church whether or not it should proceed to ordain him. This procedure allows a wider range of persons to judge his qualifications and to determine whether his understanding of Christian faith and practice is consonant with that of the denomination as a whole. The presence of such a representative group is an indication that the denomination is also conferring its approval upon the individual's qualifications for the pastoral ministry. If a single congregation should insist upon exercising its prerogative of ordination without the advice of others, then it would be logical to require the man to be reordained when, and if, he moves to another church.

The usual procedure which leads to ordination begins with licensing a man[4] to preach. This act of the local church in effect represents a notification to other churches that it would like to have them give him an opportunity to preach as occasion permits, so that his gifts can be tested. During this period he is also expected to pursue a program of study in preparation for the pastoral ministry. When his education is completed, he applies to the local church for ordination; and if the church is satisfied that he should be ordained, it notifies the association of its desire to ordain him and issues an invitation to the churches of the association to send representatives to an ordination council. The association or the state convention should arrange for a committee to examine the candidate at a preliminary meeting to see whether his credentials are in order and to determine whether or not he has met the educational and other standards that have been set by the association or the state convention. This preliminary examination of outward credentials is designed to avoid the convening of a council prematurely.

At the meeting of the ordination council, the candidate relates his Christian experience, describes his call to the ministry, and makes his own confession of faith. After this statement has been heard, and he has replied to questions put to him by the representatives of the churches, the moderator asks him to withdraw. Following a discussion of his qualifications, a vote

4 Although the word "man" is frequently used in this manual with regard to the pastoral ministry, this usage is generic, and not purely masculine. It is not intended to exclude the ordination of women.

is taken as to whether or not the council should recommend that the local church proceed with the ordination. Although there have been cases where a church has acted contrary to the advice of a council, this procedure is decidedly irregular. No such ordination should be recognized by the denomination, and the church should be asked by the association to regularize its action by referring the matter to an appropriate advisory committee or council of the association for consideration and the recommendation of appropriate steps. In some cases, this body may recommend that the earlier ordination receive associational endorsement; in others, it may recommend that the man be reordained after meeting certain requirements.

After a church has been notified of a favorable action by an ordination council, it proceeds to plan the service of ordination. Usually representatives of the association and the state convention are invited to participate in the service. The central act of ordination is the ordination prayer, in which God's blessing is invoked upon his ministry and which is accompanied by the ordained ministers present laying their hands upon the candidate. More rarely, though appropriately, one or two deacons of the ordaining church will also participate in this act. Prior to the prayer, the recommendation of the council is read, an appropriate sermon is delivered, a charge to the candidate is given, and sometimes the candidate responds by affirming vows of ordination. The ordinand is seated in the congregation, until he is requested to stand for the charge and then to come forward for the ordination prayer. Following the prayer it is customary for a welcome into the ministry to be extended to the newly ordained person, who then pronounces the benediction as the first act of his pastoral office.

Revocation of Ordination

In view of the fact that Christian ordination signifies the approval of the church for a man to serve in a specialized church calling, there should be some way to reverse the process. In some cases, men have ceased to serve as pastors and have turned to some secular employment. Sometimes, indeed, scandalous behavior has forced their withdrawal from leadership in the church. Although a church which has ordained a person may revoke that ordination, such action happens very rarely. Ordinarily, the person continues to be known as an ordained Baptist minister, no matter what is the reason for his having discontinued to serve in such a capacity. Regular procedures should be established by all associations by which an ordination can be revoked where there is no longer any reason for the person to have such approval and recognition.

Local Ministers

It should be noted here that there was a time when Baptist churches ordained a man only to a given congregation. When he moved from that congregation, his ordination ceased. If he were called to another congregation, he was ordained by that church. This was thoroughly in keeping with the Baptist understanding of the pastoral ministry, but it presented some practical problems in terms of the free movement of pastors, as the need arose, from one congregation to another. Thus the practice arose of regarding ordination as valid in all churches, with the relationship of pastor and people in a particular congregation being affirmed in a service of installation which reconfirmed the ordination for that particular church. This, on the whole, has been an eminently satisfactory procedure.

There may be some situations in which ordination should be limited to service in a particular church. There is but one ordination and there can be no different levels of privilege, status, or function of an ordained person within a local congregation. But the locale within which ordination is recognized can be, and usually is, defined with more or less specificity. It has been suggested that the ordination of a person who has met all the ordination standards of the Baptist denomination be recognized—in terms of its locale—throughout all Baptist churches. However, because many churches are unable to secure pastors who have met all the standards for ordination, some of these have either resorted to a dependence upon an irregular, unordained ministry or have proceeded to ordain a person in disregard of the established standards. To regularize this situation, it is proposed that these men be ordained as *local ministers* who, outside the context of the particular congregation by whom they have been ordained, would resume their lay status. All the privileges of the regularly ordained pastor would be accorded such a person during the tenure of his relationship to the particular congregation, but ordination as a local minister would indicate that he has not completely fulfilled the requirements for a general ordination. Such an ordination would take place following the recommendation of an ordination council. It would provide a means of establishing standards for a general ministry, without detracting from the meaning of a local ordination.

Lay Preachers

It has been further suggested that the category of *lay preacher* be restored. It is not necessary that public preaching be limited to ordained persons, but it is important that no church member should do so without the approval of the church. As the Philadelphia Confession of Faith puts it: "Although it be incumbent on the bishops or pastors of the churches to be instant in preaching the Word, by way of office; yet the work of preaching the Word is not so peculiarly confined to them but that others also gifted and fitted by the Holy Spirit for it, and approved and called by the church, may and ought to perform it." Notice especially the words, "approved and called by the church." Those so approved and called were lay preachers. There were and are many ways in which a lay preacher can be of service—for example, when a neighboring church is without a minister or when a neighboring pastor is ill. Ordination is not necessary for such a person to render acceptable service in public preaching and teaching as need arises. Even a lay preacher, however, is a representative of the church and should not exercise his gifts publicly without the approval of the church. Nor should such approval be given unless the person has the ability to perform these tasks in a creditable way. Too often a person with nothing to commend him but fluency of speech has been prevailed upon to fill a pulpit in cases of necessity. Such a relationship lacks the support and approval of the church, and demeans the office of pastor. Occasionally, the license to preach, which represents a step toward ordination, has been misused for the purpose of giving some type of certification to the lay preacher. Instead of misusing the license to preach, and instead of proceeding irregularly in allowing anyone to preach who might be asked to do so by an individual, it is suggested that churches would act much more wisely to identify those in their congregations who are capable of preaching effectively. They could be commissioned as lay preachers and would be available to fill the pulpits of neighboring churches as occasion demands.

Other Ordained Ministries

Not only pastors of congregations should be ordained. As early Baptists occasionally elected and ordained one of their number to be a ruling elder or a teaching elder, in more recent times churches have provided their pastors with associate or assistant pastors. Such persons share the pastoral responsibility and need to be ordained. Moreover, there are many who serve the churches in ways which require qualifications similar to those of a pastor. For example, the state secretaries, the executive officers of mission boards, evangelists, and professors in theological seminaries are all outside of the actual pastoral ministry. Yet they serve churches in ways similar to the duties of the pastoral office, and most of them engage to some extent in preaching and teaching. The general test as to whether ordination is needed should center upon the nature of a person's duties and his preparation. When a person serves in an office which makes him especially responsible as a guardian and transmitter of the Christian tradition and of his own denominational heritage, he should also have the kind of theological training corresponding to his work. If he serves as a representative of the churches of his denomination in such a capacity, and if he has the necessary preparation, he ought to be ordained.

VII

Other Officers of the Local Church

FEW CHURCHES TODAY ARE ORGANIZED SO SIMPLY AS TO REQUIRE no officers other than pastors and deacons. The complexity of the organization of local churches varies so much that it is difficult to make a blueprint for the structure of a Baptist church. In some cases, a church may have a staff of several persons with professional training, each of whom shares in the pastoral responsibilities, whereas the typical small congregation can support only one full-time person in the pastoral ministry. Yet even a small church today needs a number of officers to carry on its many-sided program. Considerable room should be allowed for flexibility, therefore, so that adaptations can be made to local situations.

There are some general patterns of organization, however, which characterize present-day Baptist churches. These patterns follow naturally from the practical functioning on a local level of the central mission of Christ's church. All offices and agencies of an individual church, therefore, should be kept related to the fulfillment of these functions.

1. GENERAL OFFICERS OF THE CHURCH

The Moderator. The pastor may serve as moderator of the church, or another member may be elected to serve in that capacity. Formerly, it was customary for the pastor to be mod-

109

erator, but today's practice in Baptist churches varies in this respect. There are fairly good reasons to support either plan.[1] It is also common to have the chairman of the Board of Deacons to serve in this capacity. The moderator serves as a presiding officer at the official congregational meetings, and he is an *ex officio* member of all boards.

The Church Clerk. A church clerk is essential even in the smallest congregation. Someone must keep the records. Obviously the qualifications for such an office include carefulness as to details, a sense of responsibility, and the ability to keep accurate records in legible form. Since a clerk must also carry on correspondence in the name of the church, care should be taken to select a person capable of expressing ideas in grammatically correct language. The chief duties of this office are to keep minutes of all congregational meetings, to maintain an accurate roll of the membership, and to carry on correspondence (including letters of dismission to other churches). It is also the clerk's responsibility to furnish statistical reports and other data required by the local Baptist association as well as state and national conventions. The clerk is elected by the congregation. Since there is special value in having continuity in this work, the office probably need not be rotated. Unless the incumbent is incompetent, there is no reason why he should not continue in this position indefinitely.

The Treasurer. The treasurer is expected to provide for the safekeeping and the disbursement of funds in accord with the instructions of the church. Here again accuracy and dependability are of great importance. In view of the fact that not everyone has the ability to keep careful financial records, suitable training or experience should be a factor in electing a person to take charge of this work. The records should be kept in such form that they can be easily examined by an auditing committee prior to the annual meeting of the church.

The Financial Secretary. It is usual for a financial secretary to receive and count all moneys and to deposit the receipts in

[1] See *Supra*, pp. 59-60.

the proper bank accounts. He then turns over to the treasurer a statement of such deposits. This officer keeps a record of the contributions of individual members which are given through envelopes provided by the church. At the end of the year each contributor should receive an accurate statement of his giving.

The Church School Superintendent. The general superintendent serves as the administrative head of the Sunday church school, in co-operation with the Board of Christian Education. In some churches, where there is a director of Christian education, it may be considered advisable for that person to do the work of the superintendent. The director is related to the entire educational program of the church, including vacation church school, weekday Christian education, Sunday evening programs, Sunday church school, and many other activities. When the superintendency is a separate office, this person is concerned solely with the Sunday church school, including all its departments. Too often in the past the Sunday school has acted almost independently of the church itself, choosing its own officers and having its own budget. More recently there is general recognition that this school has meaning only as an arm of the church, and acknowledgment of that fact is made when we refer to it as a Sunday *church* school. By having the general superintendent and other officers and teachers approved by the church meeting and by providing for the needs of the school through the regular church budget, the church can direct the school's affairs in a way which will best serve to fulfill its teaching ministry. When the officers of the Sunday church school are ready to assume their duties, a public installation service is appropriate to recognize that they are sharing in the teaching work of the church.

2. BOARDS OF THE CHURCH

The Board of Deacons

Whether or not the choosing of the seven to handle the common fund and serve the tables, as described in Acts 6, was the beginning of the office of deacon is a moot question. There is good reason to believe, however, that the biblical account was given for the purpose of explaining the beginning of the diaconate. In the situation depicted there, those who administered the Word (the Twelve) were being compelled to neglect their pre-eminent responsibility by becoming too involved in routine matters. Consequently, seven men were chosen from the congregation to relieve the apostles of these other duties. This step did not indicate that "serving tables" was unimportant. Indeed, the dispute which they were appointed to resolve was shattering the unity of the church. What it did mean was that those who had the special responsibility for ministering the Word should be freed to give full attention to that service for which they were best equipped. The pastoral officers should be relieved of direct management of the temporal concerns of the church which can be handled by other members.

The work of the deacons in the early church is not made very clear, although the requirements specified in 1 Timothy 3 offer some clues to their duties. They apparently were expected to have oversight over the administration of finances, and particularly to supervise the distribution of relief to the poor. In general they took charge of the temporal affairs of the churches. It is not necessary, of course, to find a pattern of activity for this office and to imitate it slavishly, but again we find guiding principles in the functions which they performed.

In keeping with the general function of the deacons, Baptists have regarded them as special assistants to the pastor. The qualifications for a deacon have been spiritual insight, trustworthiness, familiarity with the Scriptures, and administrative ability. Into their hands has fallen the task of administering funds for aiding the needy within the church family and even beyond the actual fellowship of the church members. Traditionally, they have been responsible to visit the sick, initiate disciplinary measures, prepare elements for observance of the Lord's Supper, and have general oversight of all aspects of the church's life. In the absence of the pastor, deacons have been expected to take charge of some services and to see that the pulpit is supplied. When the pastoral office has been vacant, they have provided direction for the affairs of the church.

With the multiplication of boards and committees to carry on the expanded programs of churches, there has been a tendency to diminish the area of responsibility of the deacons. Financial oversight has gradually been shifted to trustees, and special committees often look after evangelism and pulpit supply. Some churches have sought to utilize the Diaconate as the central board of the church to which all other boards and committees are subordinate, and to which all matters of vital concern to the congregation are brought for advice and approval. Other churches have preferred to limit the functions of the deacons, and instead have developed an Advisory Board or Council to co-ordinate their work. Although there are sound reasons which commend the use of the Board of Deacons as a central committee, there are also good points about the Advisory Council. Whatever a church decides, it is important that the role of the deacons be defined as clearly as possible in the church constitution.

The number of deacons necessary to a church depends upon the size of the congregation and the duties assigned to the diaconate. In a small church, two or three might be enough, whereas a larger church would need many more. If the deacons are to serve as a central committee, a larger number would be required than if their field of ministry were more narrowly defined. There should be enough so that the responsibilities which devolve upon them will not fall too heavily on individual deacons, and enough so that they can keep in touch with the entire membership.

The deacon is not usually elected for life, although some churches have followed this practice. Since problems have sometimes been created by having officers who held life tenure, most churches have now adopted a system of rotation which allows a deacon to be re-elected until he has served a specified number of years. Then he must retire and cannot be re-elected until after the lapse of a year. On the whole, results have indicated that the rotation system is superior to life tenure, assuming that other suitable persons are available for the office.

Should deacons be ordained? Such was formerly the usual practice, but there has been a tendency more recently to discard it. There would seem to be no more reason for ordaining deacons than for trustees, church school superintendent, and others. It is appropriate, however, to hold a service of recognition to install deacons as well as those elected to other offices.

There should be some women members on the Board of Deacons, although that point has been debated among Baptists. A long hesitancy to let women speak in church services kept them from serving in this capacity. In our society, however, there seems to be no good reason why women should not be deacons, and there are good reasons why they should be. Besides taking part in the regular duties of the office, there are some services which they can render better than men.

The Board of Trustees

Qualifications for the position of trustee in a Baptist church are similar to those for the deacon, and there is no warrant for the prevalent notion that spiritual discernment is less important for the former than the latter. In most states, a Board of Trustees is required by law, for property must be vested in them if a church is to be incorporated. In some churches, the deacons are designated as the trustees, but in most churches the trustees constitute a separate board.

Until legislation was enacted by the states regarding incorporation of churches, there was no office of trustee. At first, the trustees were merely figureheads, in whose names title to property was held, but gradually their responsibilities have broadened. It was natural to delegate to them responsibility for maintaining or improving church property, and ultimately many churches relegated all financial matters to this board.

Not only real estate, but securities, cash, and other church assets are under their jurisdiction.

In many churches the Board of Trustees must be consulted in all matters involving money and salaries, and in some instances they have assumed the prerogative of determining the minister's salary without action by the congregation. No doubt there must be some delegation of responsibility in this sphere, but the scope of the trustees should be clearly delimited, and care should be taken to insure that legal requirements are met.

The church constitution should indicate the work and the authority of the Board of Trustees as of other offices, and it should make clear that the decisions of trustees as of other committees and boards are always subject to approval, veto, or modification by the congregation. It is therefore important that the Board of Trustees should make complete, accurate, and regular reports to the church. Most decisions will be made within the framework of a budget adopted by the church. (See also the section on the Finance Committee, page 121.) Matters not covered by the budgetary provisions should be referred to a congregational meeting for the expression of its will.

The Board of Christian Education

Most American Baptist churches have a Board of Christian Education, designed to correlate the instructional work. It does not confine its interests to the Sunday church school, but includes within its scope of responsibilities all phases of Christian education. These include children's, youth, and adult work, as well as missionary and stewardship education and leadership education.

The Board of Christian Education will supervise and administer the entire education program in the church. The following list includes specific duties which represent the important responsibilities to be assumed by the Board:

Establish the objectives of the program
Study the needs
Determine the program

Co-ordinate activities and projects
Recruit, train, and appoint leaders
Determine the curriculum
Prepare and administer the education budget
Provide adequate rooms and equipment
Evaluate the program
Develop an educational consciousness

The size of this board will vary according to the membership of the congregation, but there should be enough persons so that attention can be given to all phases of the educational work. A minimum of six people should comprise the board; these would serve as chairman of the board, of missionary and stewardship education, of leadership education, of children's work, of youth work, and of adult work, respectively. All of these officers should be elected by the church, taking into consideration the specific responsibilities they are to exercise on the board, since they are called to do a work in which they represent the church in its teaching ministry. If there is a director of Christian education, he works in close co-operation with this board. All funds for the educational program of the church should be provided from the general treasury, and all regular offerings from the various organizations should go into that treasury.

Whatever the size of a church there is a continuing need for better prepared leaders and teachers. A chief handicap of many churches is the inadequate supply of persons who can give leadership in its diversified programs. It is possible to strengthen its leadership, however, if training is provided to equip teachers and other leaders. No person should be chosen to any position unless he is willing to give time and effort to become competent in the work associated with his office. It is the responsibility of the Board of Christian Education to see that opportunities are afforded for teachers and workers of the church to receive help which will enable them to perform their services more efficiently.

Local church programs of leadership education may deal with the content of our faith, or with teaching methods which can be individually applied to specific curriculum resources. More specialized training, such as departmental courses, can often best be done co-operatively on an association or community basis.

Therefore, the association should wherever possible serve as a unit for planning and conducting leadership training courses annually. In addition to the instruction offered locally, laboratory schools are held under denominational auspices in most states and at the national assembly. Churches should encourage their teachers to take advantage of opportunities to improve their knowledge and skills, and they should underwrite the expenses for at least one person to attend a laboratory school each year.

3. COMMITTEES OF THE CHURCH

Numerous other committees are needed for specific purposes, but their number and kind will vary with the size and needs of each church. Needless multiplication of organizations should be avoided, but there are aspects of the church's life which need the emphasis which a special committee can give to them. The duties of each committee ought to be clearly defined, and its purpose should be integral to the main mission of the church. When any organization no longer has a function which is clearly related to the purpose of the church, it should be dissolved.

Evangelism Committee. Evangelism is so closely linked with all that the church does that it cannot really be isolated as a separate activity. Yet the outreach in seeking to win men to accept Jesus Christ as Savior and Lord needs the attention of a specific committee. Through the committee the church is reminded that its mission to the world is central to its whole life. Working with other committees, boards, and auxiliary organizations, it can see that members are helped to know how they can be witnesses. The committee should also find practical ways to implement evangelistic concern. It should plan special evangelistic visitation and meetings through which the church tries to reach out to those outside of the church. It may also start mission Sunday schools where they are needed, and may help to start a new church. All appropriate means should be sought to help focus the attention of the church upon its evangelistic ministry. This committee should work in close co-operation with the Board of Christian Education.

Missions Committees. Evangelism and missions are almost the same, but the latter term stresses the fact that the church commissions some of its number to represent it in proclaiming the gospel beyond its immediate locality. "Missionary" means one who is sent, and the word conveys to our minds the thought of those who go overseas to other people, or to classes of people with special problems in our own land.

Ordinarily there are women's mission societies, but there is no good reason why missions should be the domain of women and girls. Missions are a concern of the whole church, and both men and women should be well informed about this work. Through schools of missions, women's societies, men's fellowships, youth fellowships, and adult study groups such instruction should be offered. All members should become acquainted with the philosophy of missions, the particular problems and needs of modern missions, and the work of specific mission fields.

Baptist churches have a variety of practices concerning the administration of missionary work through committees. The American Baptist Convention recommends that there be two groups—(1) a committee on missionary and stewardship education, related to the Board of Christian Education through its chairman, who is a member of that board, and (2) a committee on world mission support, related to the Advisory Council. The former is primarily concerned with educational aspects of the work, the latter with promotional and financial aspects, and the two working in close co-operation. A *Co-ordinated Plan Book,* published by the American Baptist Convention, describes this relationship and delineates the joint and separate responsibilities of the two committees.

Alternate plans found in some churches involve the use of a board of missions or a single missionary committee. In such instances, it is very important that there be close working relationships between these bodies and the Board of Christian Education.

Committee on Christian Social Concern. If the Christian is to be a witness in all of his roles and relationships, he must be able to relate his faith to social as well as personal issues. Therefore, the church program should provide information, encouragement, and channels through which the lordship of Christ may be acknowledged in family, community, nation, and world. Racial tensions, poverty and unemployment, world peace, alcoholism, narcotics addiction, religious liberty, and the ferment of revolutionary movements among peoples of other countries are a few of the problems which the Christian citizen faces. Although problems are so numerous and so complex as to make their solutions seem almost impossible, the Christian community is called to do what it can to express its answer to the perplexing questions. It cannot throw up its hands in despair and abdicate its responsibility. A church should have a committee responsible to see that relevant issues are brought to the congregation for consideration in some way. Literature can be provided for the members, and special programs can be planned where particular issues are presented and discussed. Special help is available to such committees from their denominational agencies. In the American Baptist Convention, requests for information should be addressed to the Division of Christian Social Concern, American Baptist Convention, Valley Forge, Pa. Also, the Baptist Joint Committee on Public Affairs, 1628 Sixteenth St., N.W., Washington 9, D.C., will provide materials dealing with legislation affecting religious liberty and other matters of conscience.

Communications Committee. If the members are to keep informed and in close touch with each other, good channels of communication are necessary. In part the church meeting will offer opportunity for keeping people in touch with the whole life of the church, as well as affording a means for all members to have a part in making policies and determining emphases of the church. The weekly bulletin is another means of disseminating information and keeping matters before the congregation, and preparation of this may be in the hands of a communications committee. Many churches have found it valuable to have also a bi-weekly or monthly church organ which gives an opportunity for the whole range of interests to be presented to all members of the church. The editor of such a church paper should be a member of the committee on communications. It is also the duty of such a committee to co-operate with other groups to help focus attention on special occasions and emphases, such as the school of missions, evangelistic meetings, and occasional lectures on social issues. Such a committee can help to interpret the purpose of the church to the community by means of radio, newspaper, tracts, and other means.

Nominating Committee. This committee should be appointed early in the church year, since the choice of leaders is a matter which requires careful deliberation. It may well be a standing committee of the church, so that it will be able to make plans well in advance of the election of officers, and also to make recommendations for filling vacancies created between the annual elections. In making recommendations for any office, the nominating committee should work closely with Advisory Council or Board of Deacons (whichever serves as the central committee).

Music Committee. The musical program is entrusted to the direction of this committee. The regular choir, as well as children's or youth choirs, are included within its responsibilities. Where there are paid organists, choir directors, or other music staff members, they also are under the supervision of the music committee.

Ushering Committee. Such a committee sees that ushers

are provided for the regular worship services and any other occasions when they are needed. It is responsible to see that they are properly instructed in their duties.

Finance Committee. It is the duty of this committee to prepare the annual budget to be submitted to the church, and it should work in close co-operation with the Advisory Council or Board of Deacons (whichever is the co-ordinating committee of the church) in estimating budgetary needs. In addition to compiling the budget, it should plan and direct the Every Member Canvass. Some churches also delegate to the finance committee responsibility for oversight of the disbursements during the year. Under such circumstances, it is expected to see that expenditures stay within the budget, to check income to ascertain whether or not it is in line with estimates on which the budget was based, and to make arrangements for emergency items which may arise. In other churches the supervision of disbursements is the responsibility of the trustees. Whatever plan is used, the constitution should make clear the lines of responsibility and authority.

Auditing Committee. The work of this committee is to make a check upon the financial records of the church at least once a year and report its findings to the church meeting. It should be composed of persons other than the treasurer, financial secretary, and the Board of Trustees.

Pulpit Committee. When the pastoral office becomes vacant for any reason, a committee should be elected by the congregation. The size of the committee will vary with the size of the membership, but it should be large enough to afford representation of the main aspects of the church's life. The method of selecting such a representative committee differs considerably in Baptist churches, but the individual church should provide for a clear-cut system in its by-laws. Instructions for the guidance of pulpit committees are available at state or national convention headquarters.

Other Committees. Additional committees or special organizations may become necessary to the fulfillment of a church's responsibilities, but unnecessary multiplication of agencies should be avoided. Every organized group in the church should have its objectives carefully scrutinized to see its place in the over-all purpose of the church. When societies or special agencies have outlived their usefulness, they should not be perpetuated. Those which make a significant contribution to the ministry of the church should be encouraged, but those which serve no real purpose should be discontinued. There are too many demands upon time and energy to keep alive agencies which are irrelevant to, or at cross-purposes with, the aims of the church.

4. AUXILIARY ORGANIZATIONS

Besides the church school, there are other organizations which play important roles in the nurture and training of church members. Among these are the Woman's Society, the Men's Fellowship, and the Baptist Youth Fellowship. These organizations should be the concern of the Board of Education, and they should also be represented on the Advisory Council. All church members should be considered members of these groups, and efforts should be made to enlist active interest and participation of everyone in their activities. Full information on the purpose and operation of each of these groups may be had by writing to the corresponding national office: National Council of American Baptist Women, American Baptist Men, and Department of Youth Work—all located at American Baptist Convention Headquarters, Valley Forge, Pennsylvania.

5. ADVISORY COUNCIL

Such a profusion of boards, committees, and other organizations may result in disorder, or it may become a smoothly-operating church organization. It may indeed be the means by which the gifts of the Spirit are channeled to serve the whole body. A central committee is needed to co-ordinate the diverse interests into a harmonious church program. Some churches attempt to provide such co-ordination by means of an Advisory Council or Board composed of the officers of the church and of the various organizations, while others use the Board of Deacons as a central executive committee.

There are some reasons for using the Diaconate for this function. In the first place it is an expansion of the earlier work of deacons as they were used in Baptist churches, for they were charged with assisting the pastor in general oversight of the life of the church. Assuming some administrative responsibilities and keeping in touch with the needs of the members, they freed the pastor for concentration upon his particular duties. Of more importance is the fact that the members of the Diaconate are elected by the congregation and are therefore directly responsible to it. An Advisory Council is made up of persons chosen by each agency to represent it, and only indirectly can they be said to represent the church which has not elected them to such office. Where the church makes the Board of Deacons a co-ordinating body, it assigns one or two of its members to the Boards of Christian Education and Trustees and to the major committees. In this case, when deacons are elected, it is necessary to take into account the need for having among their number persons qualified to serve on the various boards, committees, and auxiliary organizations. Also, the Board of Deacons should be large enough that responsibilities will not fall too heavily on any individual.

If the church prefers to adopt the plan of using an Advisory Council, it should make sure that this body is kept responsible to the congregation. Its decisions are subject to the veto or approval of the church. The composition of such a council includes all of the officers of the church, the chairmen of boards and committees, and the presidents of the auxiliary organizations. To such a representative group is entrusted the responsibility of overseeing the total life of the church. It sees that the many interests and responsibilities of a church are adequately provided for in the church program, and it works the varied objectives into a coherent plan. A schedule of activities for the year is arranged by this council, and long-range studies of the ministry and needs of the church come under its scrutiny.[2]

In a congregational system like that of the Baptists, authority to make policy decisions should be in the hands of the church itself. It is easy to allow authority and responsibility to slip by default into the hands of a few leaders, so that the congregation has no real voice in determining the affairs of the church. Another danger is for boards, committees, and other organizations to act with little concern for the ultimate purpose of the church of Christ. When such developments occur, they are usually the result of the unwillingness of members to accept their full responsibility. Such outcomes are a denial of the congregational principle. It is imperative, therefore, that members understand the nature and purpose of the church and the meaning of their own Christian commitment. Otherwise a congregation cannot be a real worshiping and witnessing fellowship.

If a church is to be truly a ministering fellowship, a close relationship must be maintained between worship, the church meeting, and the agencies through which it acts. Decisions are not to be made solely on the basis of personal inclinations and opinions, but with a genuine desire to express the will of our Lord. Each committee, board, and agency must see itself as expressing the life of the church, a part of the whole, and the entire congregation must be kept informed as to what is being done. As new needs and new issues are raised, there must be discussion and consideration of the responsibility of the church in these matters. Without worship, instruction, devotion, and discipline, the church can easily degenerate into a merely human organization which deals only superficially with religious matters.

    [2] For a further alternative plan, in which the diaconate is the only board, see pages 222-224.

VIII

Baptism and the Lord's Supper

SINCE THE APOSTOLIC AGE, BAPTISM AND THE LORD'S SUPPER have been recognized as practices which were commanded by Jesus Christ. By some these two acts have been called *ordinances*, while others prefer to use the term *sacraments*. Before proceeding to a consideration of baptism and the Lord's Supper, it may be useful to discuss which of these two terms should be used. Neither of them has the advantage of biblical sanction, for none of the scriptural writers employed them to refer to either of the two rites. Our judgment about these words will depend somewhat upon the way in which they are defined, but to some extent the overtones which the words carry in popular thought may make us prefer one above the other.

Baptists in general prefer to speak of ordinances rather than of sacraments. There was a time when they were less hesitant to call the Lord's Supper a sacrament, and that term is still common among British Baptists. Opposition to the latter word arose from the fact that to many it seemed to imply an almost magical conception of the bestowal of divine power.

For centuries a sacrament has been commonly defined as "an outward and visible sign of an inward and spiritual grace." In such a definition there is nothing offensive to Baptist doctrine. Usage of the term by Roman Catholics as well as by

125

some Protestants, however, conveys an impression which goes beyond that definition. It suggests that a sacrament is the means by which something is effected, and there is often a hint that God's grace is thereby dispensed by priests endowed with a special power. While official theologies may not deny the need for faith on the part of a recipient, actual practice often magnifies institutional control of God's grace and minimizes man's response.

Should a word which is so easily misunderstood be avoided? It probably should be, if there were a more suitable alternative. But the word "ordinance" is also open to misunderstanding. To call baptism an ordinance is to say that it is something ordained, or instituted, by Christ. Obedience to a command of the Lord is the primary emphasis in this term. Certainly we should give unquestioning obedience to Christ, but there is a danger that doing something for no other reason than that it is ordered may easily lead to legalism. We know that Christ had little patience with empty forms, and we may well believe that there was purpose in his bidding us to observe these special rites. In both baptism and the Lord's Supper, God's grace and man's response of faith are closely related, and we need terms which will help us to keep aware of both of these poles.

In the final analysis it is not so important which of the terms we use. We may use either of them, or we may choose to employ neither. We may think it best simply to speak of baptism and of the Lord's Supper without resorting to any word which comprehends them both. It is important, however, that we understand their purpose in order that our observance of them will be so clothed with meaning that they may speak to us. After a brief discussion of the value of symbols, we shall turn to an interpretation of these two ordinances or sacraments.

1. THE NEED FOR RELIGIOUS SYMBOLS

There is a tendency among Baptists to minimize the importance of signs and symbols, and that attitude is reflected in our approach to the two sacred observances we are considering. If a thing is only symbolic of reality, we say, why not take what is real and discard what is symbolic? Thus we may speak of baptism and the Lord's Supper as "mere symbols," and the adjective shows our low evaluation of symbols.

This disparagement of symbols indicates a lack of understanding of their value in human communication. For a sign or symbol not only points to some reality, but it may also be the means of communicating ideas and awakening responses. A symbol rings a bell, as it were, which calls to mind a whole cluster of associated events and meanings. Not only does it speak to the mind, but it calls forth emotions and may lead to decisions and actions.

Symbols as Means of Communication

Symbols are of many kinds, and they are used in all spheres of human life. We know how the American flag, under certain circumstances, may arouse deep feelings of pride, joy, patriotism, and exultation. It can do so because it brings to mind a whole series of thoughts and meanings, and thus has power to awaken a response in our feelings and actions.

Not only do symbols stir our memories and emotions, but they may be the means of transmitting something from one person to another. A handshake, for instance, is nothing more than a casual custom by which we greet acquaintances or friends. A handshake on occasion, however, communicates feelings too deep for words. When a friend has been bereaved of a loved one, and we hardly know what to say, we may grasp his hand, and in that handclasp we express unuttered thoughts and feelings. Thus a handshake communicates something of ourselves. A mother's kiss is also a symbolic act. But it is an act which conveys something of her affection and concern, and by it a child is reassured and made to feel secure. Surely we should not treat symbols carelessly, for they communicate and may even participate in the reality which they represent.

What is true in ordinary human affairs is true in the realm

of religion. Here, too, are symbols through which intangible and unseen realities are communicated to us. The power of God is mediated to men through symbols, and through such signs something of deep mystery is apprehended by us, which goes beyond our ability to explain in words. It is of such things that our fathers spoke when they talked of "the means of grace." The reading of the Scriptures, prayer, preaching, the singing of hymns, family devotions—all were regarded as means by which grace was communicated.

Baptism and the Lord's Supper as Symbols

Included among the means of grace were baptism and the Lord's Supper. These were symbols, but Baptists did not disparage them by speaking of them as "mere symbols." The same God who had deigned to act in human history, to bring the Incarnate Son of God to birth in a stable, had ordained that other elements of our common life should be means through which he acted. Through immersion in water and through the eating of simple bread and wine, men could be made more aware of God's presence and power.

It is not necessary to think of these acts as being channels through which God automatically communicates himself to those who take part in them. Baptists have always been sure that it is possible for a person to be baptized without having been affected by the experience. It is equally possible that some persons may eat and drink at the Lord's Table without being changed in any way by their act. On the other hand, these vividly symbolic actions may be the means through which the Holy Spirit speaks and acts. Therefore, they have been ordained by our Lord as special ritual observances. "By the administration of baptism and the Lord's Supper, prayer, and other means appointed of God, faith is increased and strengthened," says the Philadelphia Baptist Confession. In other words, God works through these signs. Since the same article also states that faith is wrought by the Spirit, it seems evident that baptism and the Lord's Supper were regarded as means of grace.

Although these symbols go beyond the intellect in reaching the inner depths of man's being, they have a certain intellectual content. An appreciation of their meaning is important if one is to participate in them intelligently. There is constant danger that both of these ordinances may be reduced to empty forms, and that they may be treated with indifference. Hence we should seek to understand their significance.

2. BAPTISM

The act of baptism has been interpreted in a variety of ways in the history of the church. In general there are two tendencies which characterize the diverse interpretations. On the one hand are those persons who emphasize the ceremony as a means by which God does something to a passive human being. On the other are those who stress man's active role in the baptismal act. Within the former group there is wide diversity. These viewpoints range from a belief that sins are actually washed away by this act, to the conviction that it is a sign and seal of God's covenant whereby God reassures man of the truth of his Word. Those who stress baptism as something done by men also offer several explanations. They see it as a testimony to the world, a confession to God, a means of stirring those baptized to more vivid reflection upon God's dealings with them, or a simple act of obedience to a specific command. At one extreme, therefore, are persons who believe that without baptism one is lost eternally, while at the other extreme are those who think that the act of baptism is completely unnecessary.

Baptist Concept of Baptism

While Baptists have sought to keep in sight both God's grace and man's response, the primary tendency has been to emphasize baptism as an act of obedience in which men respond to God. But even when so understood, baptism is closely related to what God has done in Christ. For what we say and do in baptism rests upon God's gracious act in Jesus Christ, and signifies our identification with him in his death on our behalf. In this way baptism recapitulates the whole Christian story and thus may become a means of grace.

Andrew Fuller, an influential Baptist theologian, described baptism as "an act by which we declare before God, Angels, and men, that we yield ourselves to be the Lord's; that we are dead to the world . . . and risen again to 'newness of life.'" Calling baptism the "initiatory ordinance of Christianity," he likened it to a soldier's oath of allegiance and to a military uniform. The analogy of an oath is a reminder that in baptism we are saying something to God, while the idea of a uniform suggests that our confession to God is made before men. By an oath a soldier pledges his loyal service to a nation, and wearing a uniform identifies him as one committed to such special service. Likewise, baptism is a means in which we yield ourselves to God, and the fact that it is done publicly makes it a sign to the world that we are members of Christ's church. Both of these aspects of baptism are essential to our understanding of it.

Thus, Baptists are numbered among those who think of baptism as primarily a response made by man. In baptism a person signifies his repentance toward God, his trust in God's mercy, and his surrender to obey God's will. As the baptism of Jesus was a public acknowledgment of his submission to the Father's will, so the Christian's baptism is a public acknowledgment of his submission to the judgment and will of God. This repentance and faith are expressed to God, but the act takes place in the presence of the church and the world. While baptism is man's response, it is closely related to the grace of God. The fact that it is a response implies that God's grace is prior to baptism, for only because God has acted in Christ is there a basis for our responding to him. It should be remembered also that baptism is the act which Christ designated as the appropriate means by which such public confession to God should be made.

The baptism which is a confession *to God before men* is more than the private affair of an individual with God. It is administered in the context of the church by whose representatives the candidate is baptized. Those who have witnessed to him and have led him to accept Christ as Savior and Lord are now administering baptism in Christ's name. In administering this rite, then, the visible church is involved as a witness both to the grace of God and to the repentance and faith of the person baptized, and it simultaneously receives him into its fellowship. He who has already been accepted by Christ into his invisible church is thus publicly admitted into the visible church in the place where he is baptized.

There has been endless debate over whether or not something is effected in an individual who is baptized. Does something happen to the person? Is he regenerated in the waters of baptism? Does he receive the Holy Spirit at that particular time? It is the view of Baptists that the baptized person has already become regenerate by the work of the Spirit prior to baptism, and that baptism is a public acknowledgment of that fact. Having already repented and confessed his faith in Christ, he has been received by Christ into his church. Now in baptism he is confessing publicly what has already been confessed in private. Therefore, the act of baptism does not make a man regenerate.

According to the record in the Book of the Acts, newly baptized persons often received an inward power which they identified with a reception of the Spirit (e.g., Acts 8:14-17; 9:17-19; 19:5-6). In at least one instance, however, people were baptized because they had already received the Spirit (Acts 10:47). Therefore, one should not link such reception inseparably to a human act which is administered by the church. That is to say, baptism is not inevitably accompanied by some purifying or renewing power of God. The church cannot guarantee that the performance of baptism will be followed by the imparting of divine grace. God's grace, or divine power, is not within the control of the institutional church, and it cannot be manipulated by its representatives.

Does it follow that nothing significant takes place in baptism? Such a conclusion is not implied in what has been said. The fact that baptism does not wash away sins, nor effect regeneration, nor necessarily bring the bestowal of the Holy Spirit, does not leave it an empty form. Indeed, baptism may and ought to be an experience of rich, spiritual blessing. When, in accord with God's command, we come before God confessing our sins, expressing our trust, and submitting our lives to holy obedience, then our lives are more open to God's activity than at ordinary times. On such an occasion one should have a heightened awareness of God's presence and power. Therefore, we may speak of baptism as a means of grace. However, we should not presume to guarantee that God will act in anyone's life simply because we have performed a particular ritual.

To regard baptism in this light keeps grace and faith in a dynamic relationship. God's grace takes the initiative, and man responds. When man responds in repentance and faith, and is receptive to God's will, there is an openness for the Spirit of God to work more freely in that life.

On the other hand, if he so emphasizes the human aspect of baptism that he loses sight of its connection with God's grace, then baptism may come to appear as a useless ceremony. Following this tendency, Baptists have sometimes treated baptism with indifference. Emphasizing the human aspect so as to separate it too much from God's grace, they have not prepared people to experience it in a meaningful way. In reacting against the claims of other people, they have often been so busy declaring what baptism is not, that they have neglected to make clear what it should be. We will do well to invest the rite with the fullness of its New Testament significance, so that it will have meaning for those who are baptized.

Baptism, then, may be thought of as a rite ordained by Christ as the means by which his disciples are to express the humble confession, the faith, and the willing obedience required of them. Jesus himself experienced baptism as a public testimony of his submission to the will of the Father, and thus instituted it as a ceremony for his church. In his final instructions to his disciples, he included "baptize" among their responsibilities, and the church understood this baptismal act to be a binding obligation upon all Christians.

The Subjects of Baptism

Inasmuch as baptism is related to repentance and faith, Baptists have normally practiced believers' baptism rather than infant baptism. They have held that New Testament examples and theological significance both favor the restriction of the rite to persons capable of making a conscious commitment. Nevertheless, during the course of history the baptism of infants became an accepted practice among Christians of other denominations, so that today the great majority of Christians have been so baptized. Therefore, Baptists have had to face the question as to whether they will give a limited approval to infant baptism. Some have taken a position that it may be defended on theological grounds as a distorted but possible form of baptism.[1]

Instead of baptizing infants, Baptists often dedicate such children to God. In such a service, parents and congregation publicly express their acceptance of the responsibility to offer every help and encouragement to their child, seeking to lead him to become a committed Christian in later years. There is value in such a special ceremony, which impresses upon home and church alike the importance of co-operation in providing Christian nurture. Nevertheless, since the dedication service involves an acknowledgment of responsibility by parents, it should be held only if at least one of the parents is known to be living a responsible Christian life. To dedicate children as a matter of course, regardless of the faith and life of the parents, would make the service an empty form.

[1] See *supra*, pp. 81-82, 83-86.

The Mode of Baptism

Baptists are also on firm ground when they insist upon immersion as the most appropriate form of baptism. That it was the usual way in which the primitive churches baptized is clearly indicated both by the use of the Greek word *baptizo* (meaning "to dip or submerge") and by the context of statements about the performance of baptism in specific cases.

Also, as a symbol it is a pictorial and dramatic representation of what is taking place. Coming before God acknowledging that we are sinners, helpless to save ourselves, we cast ourselves upon God's mercy. When we are baptized, we are not just saying that we have resolved to change our way of living. Rather, we are recognizing that our hope is in Christ. Being identified with him in his death and burial, we hope to share in the resurrection of which he was the first-fruits. It is because of Christ that we have the boldness to seek God's forgiveness and the gift of new life. Thus baptism both points to the grace of God which precedes all human action, and is a means of expressing our response to God's mercy. Besides expressing our repentance and faith, baptism also signalizes our obedience to Christ as Lord; for obedience in this act symbolizes our surrender of our total lives to follow his will.

Pointing to the central facts of the Incarnation, immersion pictorially expresses our own identification with Christ in his death, burial, and resurrection. It signifies the radical change which has been wrought by God, whereby we have become dead to sin and alive to Christ. For such a decisive event, immersion is a more expressive and appropriate form than either pouring or sprinkling. The latter methods become symbols of a symbol, and are inadequate signs of that to which they point.

Although immersion is indeed defensible as the most suitable means of baptizing, we need to be cautious not to overemphasize the amount of water used in baptism. A great deal more imagination is required to make either pouring or sprinkling symbolize an identification with Christ in his death and resurrection, but even a poor symbol may be used to express that which baptism signifies. There are undoubtedly cases where persons who are aged or infirm ought not to be immersed, and they should not be denied the opportunity to make a public confession in baptism. In such cases, pouring may be an acceptable substitute. Since the reality which is symbolized is the most important thing, and since a poor symbol may be used to express that reality, we ought not to stress the form so much as to make us lose our perspective. In our ordinary practice, however, immersion ought always to be employed.

If immersion is to be a high point of the Christian's experience, two things are necessary. First, there must be sufficient instruction prior to the act, so that the person knows what he is doing. Second, baptism should be performed with decency and care so that the experience may not be marred by awkward incidents.

Baptism should be preceded by sufficient instruction to ensure that the person baptized understands the nature and implications of the commitment which he has made. The amount of such teaching will vary according to the background of the persons involved. Usually, more time must be given to children than to adults; and more attention will be necessary for people on mission fields who are coming directly out of paganism than for those who have been reared in the church and a Christian family. Always, however, there should be a pastor's or discipleship class for the instruction of converts. The extensiveness of the training will be determined by the needs of the situation.

The Role of the Church in Baptism

Who should be the administrator of baptism? Baptists have assigned such responsibility to ordained ministers as a part of the pastoral office. For the same reason that certain other functions are delegated to such leaders, baptism ought to be performed by those who hold special pastoral office. This requirement does not imply that the pastor has any special power to effect something which others could not. It is a matter of doing things in an orderly fashion. To permit persons to baptize indiscriminately would lead to carelessness and confusion which would be injurious to the practice of baptism. There may be instances where a pastor is not available, but such cases would be most infrequent. If such should be the case, a church might appoint some deacon to baptize, but it would be preferable to seek the help of a neighboring pastor. Only if it has exhausted the possibilities of getting help should it resort to the use of unordained persons, for such a precedent opens the way to practices which could be unwholesome for the life of the church.

A question which is sometimes raised is whether a person should be baptized when he has no intention of affiliating with a local church. It is hard to conceive of a case in which such baptism would be proper. Since baptism represents public affirmation of repentance and faith, and surrender of life to God, signifying identification with Christ, it means that one is incorporated into the body of Christ. It is inconceivable that one who is becoming a member of Christ's church should not wish immediately to become a member of a visible church. Indifference toward the visible church reflects a serious lack of understanding of the nature of Christian commitment and of the place of the church in God's economy. Where such misunderstanding exists, further instruction is needed before baptism is administered. Although baptism is not primarily an initiation service, it signifies an identification with Christ which is equivalent to incorporation into his body, the church. To be received by Christ into the Church Universal should inevitably lead to identification with the visible church. For it is in and through the churches that God's Spirit especially works for man's redemption.

3. THE LORD'S SUPPER

The other ordinance, or sacrament, of the church is the Lord's Supper. Baptism is a decisive, once-for-all event, which marks the entrance into a new life in Christ. The Lord's Supper is intended to be repeated frequently, and symbolizes the sustaining of that life by Christ. One denotes the beginning of a new relationship, and the other the maintaining of a vital relationship between Christ and the church.

As in the case of baptism, the passage of time since New Testament days has brought a bewildering diversity of views among Christians in general concerning the meaning of this rite. Some believe that the bread and wine change into the actual flesh and blood of the Savior, and that the actual body of Christ is eaten. At the other extreme are those who emphasize that the elements are simply signs which remind us of bygone events. Some, therefore, expect something of an almost magical nature to take place in the ritual; others do not expect anything to happen in the eating of the bread and wine. What does the rite signify? Although there may be many facets of meaning, some one idea must be central. Only a few passages of the New Testament directly refer to this supper, several of which are parallel accounts in the different gospels. In three or four other places indirect reference is made. On the basis of very scant statements concerning this ritual, theories have been formed to interpret the rite which Christ instituted on the night of his betrayal.

Baptist Understanding of the Lord's Supper

Baptists have usually stressed the fact that the Lord's Supper is a memorial meal. Too often we have been inclined to say that it is a "mere memorial," as though it has little value for the church. To be sure, the casual way in which it is sometimes observed indicates the low regard in which it is often held. There is no reason, however, to use the disparaging word "mere" in connection with it.

Very close to the center of its meaning is the significant fact that it is intended as a memorial. To say that it is a memorial, though, does not mean simply that it points backward to ancient history. It is not just a sign which points to a historical event, as does the Fourth of July. The latter day is set apart to remind a nation of its roots; its celebration recalls a declaration of principles of freedom. The intent of such an occasion is to inspire its celebrants to similar courage and highmindedness. Something like this spirit is involved in the Lord's Supper, but the Supper is more than that.

The Lord's Supper is more nearly analogous to the Passover Feast of the Jews. That ritual meal, which was observed each year, also pointed to the past. When a family sat around the table eating, the head of the household reminded the others of the reason for its annual observance, saying in effect that this meal is a reminder of the time when the Lord God delivered their forefathers out of the land of Egypt. However, the recital of past events was not made just in order to arouse their heroism and loyalty. Reminded of what God had done once, they were to recall that the God of their Fathers was also the God of the children: "The God of Isaac and Jacob is our God." This meal was a means of helping them to maintain their identity and continuity as the covenant people of God.

In a similar way the Lord's Supper is intended to remind the church of the foundation upon which it rests, for in the Lord's Supper we see depicted the mighty acts of God in Christ. The elements of bread and wine point to the body and blood of Christ. As visible symbols which reinforce the gospel preached in words, they remind Christians of the Incarnation, of which the high points were death, burial, resurrection, and exaltation. These events signify God's deliverance of man from bondage to sin, and they recall to the church that it was Christ who was the reason for their existence. In looking back to the origins from which Christians have sprung, they remember that Christ is still their living Lord. They are encouraged to remember what God has done, in order to be made more vividly aware of what God is continuing to do, and what he has promised yet to do.

Recalling the past in order to be reminded of the existing situation is therefore more than a "mere memorial." The backward look leads immediately to the present and future. It is an important means of helping the church to remember its identity as the people of God, and Christ's promise to be with them to the end of the age. The remembrance of what God has done is thus a preparatory step to a fresh confrontation with the living God who is in their midst working out his purposes in and through them. It reminds them of their dependence upon the Lord Jesus Christ, who is the Bread of Life by which its life must be sustained daily.

Close to the center of the meaning of this memorial rite are four related ideas: covenant, church, Christ, and communion. Pointing to the work of the incarnate Christ, Christians speak of the New Covenant sealed with his blood. "This cup is the new covenant in my blood" (1 Cor. 11:25), Jesus is reported to have said to his disciples, as he bade them to drink it. This covenant, like that with Israel, is not an agreement between equals, but an offer made by God to men who could not save themselves. It was an offer of pardon and power which could be freely received by those who were willing to accept it with gratitude and faith.

The mention of the covenant immediately suggests a people who are the covenant people of God, the church. As Israel was constituted through the Old Covenant, so the church is the people whose existence rests upon the New. When the people of the church gather around the Lord's Table, therefore, they partake of a covenant meal, by which they are reminded of their identity as a people called by God, his purchased possession, and an instrument for his purpose.

At the head of this church, or covenant people, is Jesus Christ the Lord. He who once lived among men in a visible form is now in the midst of his people wherever they are gathered. The Holy Spirit makes Christ contemporary to each gathered congregation in every generation. To meet together and be reminded of their identity as a covenant people is to recognize the real presence of Christ in their midst; it is to remember that God always stands over against them in judgment and in mercy.

The church so gathered and so engaged is in communion with one another and with Christ. Partaking of the meal is a reminder that they are participants in the new life in Christ, that they are not isolated individuals each in search of God in his own way, but sharers in the fellowship of the Spirit. "The cup of blessing which we bless," wrote Paul, "is it not a participation in the blood of Christ? The bread which we break, is it not a participation in the body of Christ? Because there is one loaf, we who are many are one body, for we all partake of the same loaf" (1 Cor. 10:16-17).

In this service as in baptism, God's grace and man's faith are in close union. The elements of the supper depict in vivid fashion the redemptive action of God in Christ. By them we are reminded of the Incarnation—the life, death, resurrection, exaltation, and promised return of Jesus Christ. This look at what took place in history reminds us that these events have become a part of our own history, for we have accepted the free forgiveness of God and have responded to his call to be his people. We are reminded who we are and what we are to be and to do. United with Christ and with one another, we are not a loose collection of individuals but a fellowship of believers who have a corporate existence as the church of Jesus Christ.

To see in this supper, then, a memorial rite is not to rob it of meaning. A service which helps the church to a realization of its own identity and reminds it of its call to live responsibly before Christ has significance. Although it is primarily a memorial symbol, emphasizing covenant, church, Christ, and communion, there are many other derivative ideas associated with it. Surely it is an occasion for rejoicing and for thanksgiving—it is thus a eucharist.[2] Although it is not a re-enactment of the sacrifice of Christ, but a reminder of the sacrifice offered by him once-for-all, it does become a time when we offer ourselves anew to God. While not primarily an occasion for seek-

---

[2] From the Greek *eucharistos*, meaning "grateful."

ing forgiveness of sins, it does invite self-examination and repentance.

When the Lord's Supper is observed as it should be, it leads to fresh encounter between Christ and his people. No more than in baptism can we manipulate or dispense God's grace, for his divine power is beyond our control. Nevertheless, in the moment of our remembering who we are as the church of God, our spirits are quickened. As we remember what God has done, what he continues to do, and what he will do, our consciousness of the divine presence is strengthened. If God thus vouchsafes to us the assurance of his presence and power, this service becomes for us a means of grace.

Early Baptists had a conception of the Lord's Supper which made its character as a memorial pre-eminent, but they also believed that Christ was truly present to the believers in that meal. The Particular Baptists expressed their view of the Lord's Supper as something more than a look back to past events. In the supper, they averred:

Worthy receivers, outwardly partaking of the visible elements in this ordinance, do then also inwardly by faith, really and indeed, yet not carnally and corporally but spiritually, receive and feed upon Christ crucified and all the benefits of his death—the Body and Blood of *Christ,* being then not corporally or carnally but spiritually, present to the faith of believers in that ordinance, as the elements themselves are to their outward senses.[3]

Here is the backward look, but its purpose is to remind of present relationships and responsibility. Participation in the Lord's Supper rekindles faith and results in a fresh meeting between Christ and his church.

Some Practical Questions Regarding the Lord's Supper

A number of practical questions relative to the observance of the Lord's Supper frequently arise. How often should it be celebrated? Is it to be confined to the use of a local congregation, or can it be held in larger gatherings? Should the ele-

[3] Lumpkin, *op. cit.,* page 293.

ments be taken to private homes for observance of the rite? Should the administration of this ordinance be only by ordained persons? Is open or closed communion more consistent with our Baptist doctrine?

The Lord's Supper is a church ordinance, and we must be careful to see that its observance is consistent with its meaning and purpose. However, Christ gave little or no instruction about the way in which it should be conducted. Therefore, we must make our deductions about this service from our understanding of the church and of the nature of this ceremony.

Above all, the connection of this supper with the church should be kept in sight. As the Passover Feast was linked to the Israel of the Old Covenant, so the Lord's Supper is closely associated with the church as God's covenant people. This rite signifies the New Covenant ratified by Christ's vicarious death, and its observance should always be such that it will emphasize the presence of Christ in his covenant community. As these central factors are kept clear, the covenant meal will contribute to the deepening of the fellowship within the Christian community, as the members look to Christ the head of the church.

The Lord's Supper ought always to be an integral part of the worship service and should be accompanied by the preached word. The bread and the cup are visible signs which represent the same thing as the preached gospel, and the visual elements and the actions serve to reinforce the preaching. To separate the Supper from the sermon is to invite a superstitious attitude toward the rite, for history has demonstrated the ease with which people can give an almost magical meaning to it. It is not a sacred mystery in which some divine power is imparted by the very eating and drinking. No attempt should be made to create an atmosphere of deep solemnity, which would invest this occasion with some dignity different from that of other worship services. There should be a quiet reverence in any meeting where a congregation gathers to worship the Lord, but no extra solemnity should characterize this service. Indeed it is a joyous occasion, and a time of thanksgiving, when God's people join in a meal reminding them of their origins and purpose.

There is no rule about the frequency with which the Supper should be observed. Baptist practice has varied from holding it every week to holding it every quarter of a year. There are good reasons for observing it each week, but considerations of time make that frequency difficult. Also, it is true that something repeated too often may lose its power to speak to us. Probably once a month is a suitable practice. The important thing is that it should be held regularly and that careful attention be given to interpret its meaning to a congregation.

Should the Lord's Supper be confined to the local church? There are many who would so restrict it, but there is no good reason for such a limitation. If the church were visible only in local congregations, there would be grounds for saying that the local church is the only place to celebrate such a church ordinance. However, the church is larger than the local congregation, and the representatives of churches gathered in a meeting may also be considered the church.

Nevertheless, when we have agreed that there are other places where the Lord's Supper may legitimately be held, the question will be raised as to where the lines are to be drawn. Should a pastor carry a little bag which contains bread and wine and administer the Supper to his parishioners in the hospital and in the homes? Some Baptists have begun such a practice in imitation of other denominations. The practice of holding communion services for a wedding party or other special gathering has not been unheard of, and communion services have been held at men's or women's meetings. It was once Baptist practice in some areas to have a communion service at an associational meeting, and on occasion special services are held at a seminary or college. Are all of these appropriate or not?

After considerable study of the Lord's Supper, a group of

British Baptists concluded that "occasional communion" was proper under certain circumstances other than in local churches. They formulated principles which would guide them in determining when such a service would be appropriate. The first requirement is that a gathering of Christians should be very clearly met for such purposes as indicate the churchly character of their meeting. Second, the meeting should be of a kind where it is fitting that those present should profess their Christian faith and obedience in an act of corporate worship at the Lord's Table. Third, the situation should be such that the observance can be carried on in reverence and seriousness.

Accordingly, an associational meeting might be a very appropriate place for holding the Lord's Supper; so might a state or national convention, although the difficulties of having a reverent service in a convention hall might present a problem. Whether men's brotherhoods or women's groups should meet for communion breakfasts is a question which would have to be decided on the basis of the tests listed above. Hard and fast rules cannot be made for such matters. However, it is not at all appropriate for a private couple or a wedding party to have a service of this kind.

There still remains the question of taking communion services to those who are ill at home or in the hospital. Is such a practice appropriate? If this is an ordinance intended to deepen the church's experience of Christ's presence and to strengthen its sense of identity as the church, then the pastor should not carry a little container around to serve communion personally to individuals. Not only does such a practice convey a false idea of the church; it also tends to encourage superstitious reverence for the Lord's Supper, obscuring its real intent.

However, there are undoubtedly persons who by circumstances beyond their control are deprived of an opportunity to participate in the services of the church. It would seem that some provision should be made to extend the fellowship of the church to them beyond the walls of a meeting house.

Therefore, it is proper for services to be held in the home of a shut-in, if proper care is taken to make this a service of the church. The pastor ought not to go to such an occasion alone, but should take the deacons and perhaps others who represent the church. In connection with the service, there should be a prayer, a Scripture lesson, and a brief message which will interpret and prepare for the memorial meal. When thus safeguarded, the Lord's Supper is kept in line with its intent.

Whether there should be an ordained minister officiating at such a service is another practical question. Baptists have usually insisted that unless such an ordained person was present there should be no observance of the Lord's Supper. Indeed, there are instances in which Baptist churches have gone for a year or two without such an observance because there was no pastor who could conveniently be with them for the occasion. Such a circumstance would not be likely today, for there is usually someone near enough at hand to help in such a matter.

The reason for insisting upon ordination as a requisite for administering the Lord's Supper is to keep it from being treated carelessly. Baptists have felt that allowing other persons to lead such a service could set a precedent which would open the door to anyone to do so. However, it does not seem necessary to be so strict that no exceptions can be made to the general rule. Certainly the church is responsible to see that due seriousness and reverence are shown toward the observance, and it carries out that responsibility in part by delegating the leadership of the service to a proper person. Ordinarily the pastor or another ordained man should conduct the Lord's Supper, and it is rare that provision cannot be made to get outside help. However, in cases of necessity, a church may vote to approve some unordained man to take charge—a deacon or a theological student not yet ordained, but already preaching. In such cases, care should be taken to select someone who is fitted in spirit, character, and ability to take the lead in a service of this kind.

The question of open or closed communion once agitated the Baptist churches deeply. Until the last decade or two of the nineteenth century, very few Baptist churches would allow persons who had not been immersed upon a profession of faith to take communion with them. They reasoned that baptism ought to precede participation in the Lord's Supper; all churches, they said, hold that unbaptized persons must not take communion. However, as Baptists saw the matter, pedobaptists are not really baptized. Therefore the churches felt they had no alternative but to refuse to join with such people at the Lord's Table.

This refusal was often a matter of regret and of embarrassment to Baptists. They were troubled about their practice of closed communion, for they regarded as Christian brethren many whom they could not admit to their communion service. Sometimes, even a man of another denomination who supplied their pulpit was unable to share in the communion service.

Gradually there has been a breaking away from closed communion, for there does seem to be an inconsistency in refusing to commune with those whom we believe to be fellow-Christians. There are two grounds on which open communion may be rationalized. On the one hand, one may say that there is no biblical requirement which stipulates that one must be baptized prior to taking part in the Lord's Supper. Therefore those who give evidence of being Christians may come to the Lord's Table even though they are not really baptized. By an alternative line of reasoning, one may say that although infant baptism is not baptism, yet infant baptism plus confirmation may be accepted as a faulty form of baptism. On either of these bases one may argue for open communion. At any rate there is a discrepancy between accepting persons as brothers and sisters in Christ but refusing to sit at the Lord's Table with them. In the North the practice of open communion is now almost universal among Baptists, and in many parts of the South it is also common.

CONCLUSION

Thus Baptists have their own traditional views of the two ordinances, or sacraments. While they are not sacramentalists, their interpretations do allow room for considering baptism and the Lord's Supper, under proper circumstances, as means of grace. The use of the term "ordinance" emphasizes that these two observances are based upon commands of Christ. However, God's grace and man's faith are closely related in both of these rites; and, when properly observed, either occasion should bring a heightened experience of God's presence and power. Therefore they may be called sacraments, provided that this word is properly defined. In order to avoid misunderstandings which grow out of the associations connected with the terms "ordinance" and "sacrament," one may simply speak of baptism and the Lord's Supper by their own names, and ignore both of the other designations. It should always be kept in mind that both rites are intimately related to the life of the church. They are to be performed only within the context of its fellowship and by its authorized representatives.

IX

The Baptist Association

IN AN EARLIER CHAPTER, REFERENCE WAS MADE TO THE TENSION existing between the idea of the universal church and that of individual local congregations. In attempting to define the relationship between these two entities, some Protestants had separated them in such a way as to set them in contrast to each other. The universal church was treated as so invisible that it had little bearing upon the actual churches; local congregations, on the other hand, were so strongly emphasized as to make the universal church seem to be nothing more than a pure abstraction.

Early Baptists tried to avoid such a sharp cleavage. They maintained first of all that "the holy catholic church" becomes visible in particular churches. According to this concept, each congregation of professing Christians is an outcropping of the larger church, the local expression of the larger church. By attempting to maintain regenerate church membership, these Baptists of earlier days sought to make the composition of the particular churches approximate that of the church as it was known to God. To each such congregation, they said, God has given all power necessary for ordering its life under the headship of Christ. Yet they recognized that the church as a whole was greater than any local congregation.

1. THE ASSOCIATIONAL PRINCIPLE

Interdependence of Churches. A further step had to be taken, therefore, to make plain the relationship between universal and particular churches. Some safeguard was needed to prevent an excessive stress upon local independence from obscuring the unity of the church. Local churches were not regarded as isolated units, but rather they recognized themselves as integral members of the total church which is the body of Christ. The earliest London Baptist Confession of 1644 pointedly expresses a sense of interrelatedness: "Though we be distinct in respect of our particular bodies, . . . yet are all one in communion, holding Jesus Christ to be our head and Lord." Other statements in the various confessions support this conception of unity which was held by Baptists.

It was necessary to give more than verbal assent to the idea of unity among the churches. Some visible means of expressing the relationship and mutual concern of the particular churches was needed, and for that purpose the Baptists devised the association. The term "association" did not come into use as a common designation for the formal connectional life for a few years; at first, Baptists preferred to speak of "general assembly" or "general meeting." However, both General and Particular Baptists had begun the development of an associational life by 1660.

Early Beginnings of Associations. The associational principle was strong in Baptist life both in England and America. The association met practical needs, and it was rooted in the Baptist view of the church. In 1652, the Berkshire Baptists stated their associational principle as follows: "There is the same relationship betwixt particular churches each towards other, as there is betwixt particular members of one church, for the churches of Christ do all make up but one body or church in general under Christ their head." [1] In England these organiza-

[1] E. A. Payne, *The Baptists of Berkshire through Three Centuries,* Appendix I, pages 147 ff. London: Carey Kingsgate Press, 1951. Cited by Hugh Wamble, "The Beginnings of Associationalism among English Baptists," *Review and Expositor,* Oct., 1957, page 547.

tions served as means of distributing benevolences, constituting new churches, resolving disciplinary problems, settling questions of theology and polity, and eventually of controlling ordination.

2. THE PHILADELPHIA BAPTIST ASSOCIATION

A look at the formation and activities of the Philadelphia Baptist Association affords an idea of the way in which such an organization was conceived. Organized in 1707, it was the parent stem from which the major Baptist bodies in America have sprung. The fact that it did not begin until that date has led some interpreters to the mistaken conclusion that the associational idea was something which independent churches developed only gradually. Actually, however, the General Baptists had formed an association, or general assembly, in New England by 1670. Most of the early New England Baptists were of that persuasion and most of them therefore belonged to that body.

Prior to 1690 the Particular Baptist churches in America were too few and scattered to have an associational life. By that date, there were four Baptist churches in the middle colonies, and they had begun informal meetings together. In 1688, the Pennepack Baptist Church came into existence, and shortly thereafter there were three others in neighboring New Jersey: Middletown (1688), Piscataway (1689), and Cohansey (1690). These churches held joint meetings for the purpose of administering baptism, ordaining ministers, and providing inspiration. A few years later the Welsh Tract Baptists formed a church. In 1707, these five Particular Baptist churches formed the Philadelphia Baptist Association.

Until the second half of the century this was the only association among the Particular Baptists in America, and it came to include member churches from the colonies in the North and South. When other associations were formed, they followed the pattern of the Philadelphia Baptist Association and were affiliated with it.

The Role of the Philadelphia Baptist Association

How did this early association conceive its nature and function? It is difficult for Baptists today to realize the strong corporate sense of the Baptists in that day. Accustomed to more individualistic ideas, we may too easily read into the earlier terms "independence" or "particular churches" some modern ideas of "the autonomy of the local church."

In their theory of the association, Baptists tried to steer a course between the extremes of overemphasizing or underemphasizing the place of the local church. While acknowledging their belief in "the catholic or universal church," they also stressed the importance of the local congregation. The particular churches, they maintained, represented the larger church and had all the powers belonging to the larger Christian fellowship. On the other hand, along with this recognition of the significance of particular churches, there was an equal insistence upon their interdependence. Such churches, declares a manual of discipline issued in 1743 by the Philadelphia Baptist Association, "may and ought to maintain communion together in many duties which may tend to the mutual benefit and edification of the whole." Thus, their thinking about the association simply reiterated that of the English Baptists in the seventeenth century.

We may learn more about their viewpoint from "An Essay on the Power and Duty of an Association," which was approved by the Philadelphia Association in 1749. Beginning with the assertion that "an association is not a superior judicature," this document proceeds to assert the powers which belong to the local church under Christ. However, the statement also adds: "Yet we are of opinion that an association of the delegates of associate churches have a very considerable power in their hands, respecting those churches in their confederation." What they regarded as independence of the churches was balanced by a strong sense of interdependence.

Although the association had no legal control over the churches, the representative body had an authority of its own.

Admittedly, an association could not interfere directly in the affairs of a congregation. It could not, for example, discipline a member in one of the churches. If a member of a particular church needed to be disciplined, however, the association could recommend that he be dealt with in a disciplinary way. The church was then expected to heed that advice, and if it refused to do so it might be excluded from the association. The relationship of the association toward its member churches was explained in the "Essay" as analogous to that of a church to its members: "But in the capacity of a congregational church, dealing with her own members, an association, then, of the delegates of associate churches, may exclude and withdraw from defective and unsound or disorderly churches."

Thus the association could not dictate to the churches what they were to do, but churches were expected to seek the counsel of the association in difficulties and to respect the judgment of the delegates. Although that body had only limited powers of enforcement, the power to expel uncooperative members constituted an important authority. Since the Baptist doctrine of the church obligated a congregation to be associated with other churches, it was important to keep the associational connections intact. To be forced out of the larger fellowship would deprive it of needed encouragement and help, and to live in isolation was a virtual denial of its doctrine concerning the unity of the church.

Examination of the records will reveal that these early Baptist churches felt an obligation to hold fellowship with one another. They united in associations where they could cooperate in matters of mutual interest and in the furtherance of the gospel. There was no thought of living in isolation, for each church was representative of a larger whole.

A look at the activities of the Philadelphia Baptist Association shows how diverse and broad were its concerns. In general terms its aims were "to consult about such things as were wanting in the churches, and to set them in order." Whatever touched the life of individual churches or affected their common witness came within the scope of its interest.

In keeping with the aim of having an informed membership in the churches, this association considered the edification of the churches as one of its major aims. It was to that end that several sermons were preached at the regular meetings. Circular letters were sent out to the churches from the association, dealing with points of doctrine or practice. The association also served as a forum where doctrinal or practical questions might be discussed. In order to encourage the development of an informed constituency, the association published printed materials such as its confession of faith, the *Treatise of Discipline*, a catechism for children, and a hymnal.

A second important purpose was the provision of a suitable ministry for the churches. Churches which were "destitute" of a minister would be provided with supply preachers, and arrangements were made for them to observe the Lord's Supper. To guard churches against unqualified persons who claimed to be Baptist ministers, the Philadelphia Association asserted the right to examine and certify "all gifted brethren and ministers that might come in here from other places." It also urged churches to seek out young men with promising talents for the ministry, and then took steps to make it possible for such persons to receive a proper education. This interest in education ranged from the use of educational funds to the establishment of a college.

Third among the general aims of the Philadelphia Association was the maintenance of peace among the churches. From the beginning it claimed the right to hear appeals from aggrieved members of churches, and to give advice in the settling of disputes. Initiative could be taken where churches seemed to be in distress, as illustrated by this entry from the *Minutes* of 1731:

The associated brethren seeing no messengers from Piscataqua as usual, and hearing by some of our brethren of the sad and distracted condition of that congregation, they thought proper to write to them, and to appoint Mr. Jenkin Jones and Mr. Joseph Eaton to give them a visit before winter, which by the blessing of God, proved a means to reduce that church to peace and order.

It should not be necessary to add that the association could not coerce a church or impose a decision upon it; it could, however, determine and declare its convictions. When the association has expressed itself, says the *Treatise of Discipline:* "the churches will do well to receive, own, and observe such determinations."

Another aspect of its work had to do with the forming of new churches. Representatives of the association were sent to the South on more than one occasion. Later in the century support was raised for missions to the Indians. After the establishment of William Carey's mission in India, the association encouraged an interest in foreign missions.

As the number of churches increased, it became necessary to form other associations. The first of these was the Charleston Baptist Association, in South Carolina, in 1751, when there were four Baptist churches in that vicinity. Before long there were associations in Virginia and in New England. The new associations were modeled after the Philadelphia pattern. Part of the intention was that the associations themselves should be affiliated with one another in order to maintain unity among the Baptist churches. With the rapid Baptist growth after the Revolutionary War, however, it was difficult to maintain this relationship, and greater diversity in practice and doctrine began to develop.

The Decline of Associations

Inevitably, changes occurred. In the nineteenth century, a number of forces wrought some alterations in the Baptists' self-understanding. Partly because of a prevailing climate of opinion which favored individualism, the independence of the local church was exaggerated to the point of weakening the sense of interdependence. Under the impact of varied cultural and regional influences, the Baptists deviated in many respects from their own tradition. The need for many ministers, to meet the rapid expansion of the churches, led to the ordination of men who were often unfamiliar with Baptist theology and history. Without properly prepared pastoral leaders, the Baptists gradually underwent many changes which eventually threatened a loss of their sense of identity.

One of the changes which took place by the end of the nineteenth century was the dwindling of the association's importance. Partly because of the rise of independent voluntary societies for special purposes, and partly because of the development of state conventions, the association was robbed of its normal functions. In most cases the association survived only to provide inspiration at an annual meeting, although in the middle of the twentieth century some efforts were being made to revive the association as a significant feature of Baptist life.

3. THE ROLE OF ASSOCIATIONS TODAY

It is clear that the association should have an important place in the life of the churches, forming a bridge between the local churches and the state and national conventions. Comprising a number of churches, the association makes available combined strength and wisdom which can supplement the resources of a local church. Through consultation and co-operation, each congregation can be strengthened and mutual tasks can be undertaken more efficiently. At the same time, the nearness of the association to the grass roots affords a familiarity with the needs of the local situation which is often lacking in those who are more remote from it.

In many matters of importance to the member churches, the enlistment of local leadership in the area served by the association will bring about more realistic planning and greater effectiveness in results than is otherwise possible. The association serves as a means of information and inspiration, and through delegates the churches can also participate in making policies. Evangelistic and missionary interests can be promoted, leadership training courses held, and new churches established through committees of the association. In matters of social concern, the churches can work together to achieve desirable ends. Standards of ordination can be determined also, although an association should take such steps in co-operation with the state and national conventions to assure uniformity among the various associations, with respect to requirements. In many ways the recovery of a wholesome associational life can result in greater stability and efficiency, and it will be a check against the concentration of power in a few hands which would take all responsibility from the local churches.

Committees Preferable to Councils

Councils, formerly needed for considering some inter-church problems, are no longer necessary. The purposes once served by councils may now be met by the association through its permanent and special committees. The term "council" meant a gathering of representatives from neighboring churches, who had been invited by another church to advise it on some question or problem. Such meetings were extra-associational; they were called to meet a particular situation and were dissolved when their work had been done. Originally, the council was useful because distance made it difficult to convene a special meeting of the association when some urgent matter demanded attention. Later, when a growing sense of independence had begun to obscure the values of the association, the council was preferred as a substitute for the association's more direct action. The ephemeral character of the former seemed to constitute a better protection of the autonomy of the local church than did a more permanent body.

Both on practical and theological grounds there is good reason to work through the association. From the standpoint of convenience the council is no longer needed, for modern transportation makes it easy for associations to assemble at frequent intervals. In a day when most churches are separated by no more than an hour's travel time, matters once referred to councils can now be handled by the association or its committees. Moreover, we now realize that the excessive concern for the autonomy of the local church which fostered the council after the need for it had ended represents a misunderstanding and perversion of the true nature of the church. The association, with its committees, represents all the churches, and its orderly procedures give more stability and continuity to church policies than would be possible with independent councils.

Associations and Ordination

For example, the association should take responsibility for determining the fitness of a candidate for ordination. The earliest examples of ordination procedures indicate that Baptist churches felt obliged to consult others in such an important matter. In the Philadelphia Baptist Association, representatives of the churches were always involved in the examination and ordination of a candidate. No church would have thought of ordaining anyone to the ministry without the assistance of other congregations. The Charleston Baptist Association, the second associational body in America, followed the parent group in this procedure. When asked by a member church about the method of ordination, it advised, "that the church call in the assistance of at least two, but rather three, of the ministers in union, who are the most generally esteemed in the churches for piety and abilities."

Even as late as the middle of the nineteenth century when connectional bonds were becoming looser, President Francis Wayland, a strong proponent of local church autonomy, wrote: "A single church does not ordain; it calls a council, generally representing the churches in the vicinity, who are present by their minister and such private brethren as they may select."[2] The ordination of a minister was so obviously a matter of concern to others than the local church that a representative

---

[2] *Notes on the Principles and Practices of Baptist Churches,* page 114. New York: 1857.

group was expected to take part in the examination and in the ordination service.

Applying this principle to present-day conditions, Baptists now find that it is best to work through regular associational channels rather than to depend upon *ad hoc* assemblies chosen on the basis of the conveniences of the moment. Although the local church retains its authority to ordain a person, it submits his qualifications to the representatives of sister churches for consideration and advice. While this examining group may still be termed a "council" if so desired, its structure should consist of delegates from the churches in the association. The association ought also to have a permanent committee which can make a preliminary examination of the credentials of the applicant. Furthermore, the invitation to the churches to send delegates to a meeting to examine the candidate should be sent out by the association. When an examining group has reached a decision regarding the suitability of a candidate, it recommends that the church to which he belongs proceed with a service of ordination or it advises against such action.

On some occasions, churches have ordained persons contrary to the advice of the examining body. There is no legal power to prevent such a course of action, but if a church ignores the judgment of the representatives of the association, the ordination should be declared invalid. Notice of such action should be reported to the state and national conventions, and no denominational listing should include the name of that person unless he has been subsequently ordained by regular procedures.

Associations and New Churches

The formation of a new church is another occasion where councils were once used, but where a representative associational committee is more suitable today. In the past, when a new congregation was to be constituted, it was customary for representatives of neighboring churches to take part in the organizing process. A committee representing the churches ascertained the qualifications of those who presented themselves as charter members and made an examination of their doctrinal standards. It was not unusual to have the constituent members publicly sign a confessional statement and a covenant in affirmation of their faith.

When the credentials had been pronounced satisfactory, a formal service was held during which the group was declared a Baptist church. The report of the organization of a Baptist Church at Cape May, New Jersey, in 1712, provides an illustration of such a process. The pastor and two elders from the Cohansey Baptist Church were invited to assist in the constituting of the church. After the statements of the constituent members had been declared satisfactory and the proposed documents had been scrutinized, the visiting minister signed the following article: "Inasmuch as you have covenanted to walk together in church fellowship according to Gospel institution; we do in the presence of God declare you to be a church of Jesus Christ; . . . We subscribe ourselves . . . on behalf of the Cohansey Baptist Church."

The procedure for constituting a Baptist church today varies in details, but the principles are those which have guided Baptist practice in the past. Whereas it was once more convenient to leave such matters to councils, it is now considered better to have a committee representing the churches of the association to perform the work of examining credentials. If the associational representatives are satisfied with their findings in this examination, they will then approve the newly formed group as a Baptist church. A public service should then be held to recognize the fact that a new church has been organized. It would be appropriate at that time to have the originating members give public assent to their articles of faith and publicly to recognize their covenant obligations.

Associations and Church Disputes

One other kind of situation in which councils were frequently useful in past years was the settlement of disputes.

Many are the cases on record where internal strife has attracted the attention of sister churches, and a council was called for the purpose of arbitration. Usually the council was called at the behest of the church involved, but sometimes the association took the initiative. On other occasions, an aggrieved member brought his case to the attention of the association, and sometimes a council was called to deal with a church which had received into its fellowship someone who had been excluded by another church.

Today the idea of having delegates from various churches consider the internal affairs of any one church sounds strange. To resort to such a means of settling problems would be regarded by Baptists generally as an infringement upon the autonomy of the local church. However, there is good reason why an associational committee should be asked to help a church in the decision of difficult points. Often there is need for disinterested parties to enter into the dispute and help the opposing factions to arrive at an amicable settlement. In many cases, where churches have been torn apart by strife, intervention by the association to which they belonged would have been both wise and proper. It is unfortunate that our individualistic interpretations of the local church have resulted in the disappearance of such procedures. Although there would be difficulties in recovering such a practice, it accords well with traditional Baptist usages and with our conception of the church.

Relationships with the Association

There is a wide range of interests in which associational committees, either permanent or special, might serve the churches well in our day, fulfilling the same functions and values as the councils once did. It should be recognized, of course, that the association is the servant and not the master of the churches; it does not have inherent power in its own right, but is the creature of the churches. Its advice should be listened to with respect, although its decisions have only a moral authority. The decisions made by a carefully selected, representative group of Baptists are more than mere irresponsible opinions. Rather they offer the combined judgment of persons of integrity. A church therefore should not disregard the judgment of the association without the best of reasons for doing so.

A strong associational life would not eliminate the need for state and national conventions. There are many areas which cannot be the direct responsibility of churches at the local level, because of the needs for specialists and administrators to formulate and execute policies. Among these specialized fields are home and overseas missions, Christian education, higher education, and publications.

The churches can share responsibly in these areas, however, if a representative system is developed which would send delegates from the associations to the state and national conventions. With churches informed about issues, and delegates instructed as to the thinking of the churches of the association, it would be possible for the churches to have an effective voice in major decisions which affect the life of the denomination.

X

Regional and National Organization

BAPTISTS IN AMERICA HAVE FOUND TENSION BETWEEN localism and the wider church most acute at the national level. As regional and national organizations have expanded to meet changing circumstances, a sense of alienation between local churches and those who were engaged in mission at a national level has increased. Especially, when structures have not provided for participation in the larger work, the gap has increased between the grass roots and those in national offices.

As long as the mission of the church was narrowly defined, a loose-knit federation of churches was adequate to accomplish goals requiring cooperation. That is not to imply that when organization was simple, there was complete absence of friction. Even when "associations" were the only form of organization beyond the local congregation, there were sometimes conflicts over the boundaries of associational authority. On the whole, however, associations did serve almost universally to enable churches to maintain doctrinal unity, provide fellowship, supply a ministry, and work together in a few common undertakings. As churches multiplied and membership grew, and the concept of the churches' purpose was enlarged, the need for additional organization increased, offering more opportunity for conflict.

163

In the nineteenth century, Baptists who had heretofore thought of themselves as churches of "like faith and practice" began to become fragmented. In some cases, such as the Primitive and Landmark Baptists, division resulted from tension between local autonomy and the claims made by mission societies and conventions. Other breaches came about over slavery, the desire of Freedmen to have their own churches, the inclination of ethnic groups to maintain their identity, and controversies over doctrinal differences and personal clashes over leadership. As a consequence of repeated separations, the *Yearbook of American and Canadian Churches* now lists twenty-five Baptist bodies in the United States.

Although sharing a common heritage of doctrine and practice, the various groups of Baptists have developed diverse patterns of organization, especially beyond the levels of local churches and associations. Therefore, while the basic principles outlined in a manual of polity, such as this, may apply to most Baptists, specific descriptions of organization are not uniform enough to be applicable to all groups. As one moves from the association to state and national levels, the differentiation of organizational forms becomes more apparent. The American Baptist Churches in the U.S.A.[1] differs greatly from the Southern Baptist Convention, and neither of these is very similar to any of the other larger Baptist bodies. Consequently, in this chapter, attention will be focused upon the American Baptist Churches (ABC/U.S.A.), tracing the stages by which the present shape has been attained.

The ABC/U.S.A. has developed a more cohesive pattern of organization than has any other Baptist body in the United States. Beginning with a very loose congeries of associations, state conventions, and societies for missions,

---

[1]Called the Northern Baptist Convention at its inception in 1907, and renamed American Baptist Convention in 1950, this denomination adopted the name "American Baptist Churches in the U.S.A." in 1972.

education, publication, and evangelism, it has moved to a system in which the relationships between the various parts are clearly defined and lines of authority and responsibility are distinguished. This outcome is the result of a desire for a polity, or pattern of organization, which would facilitate the work of the churches in fulfilling their vocation as the Body of Christ.

Remodeling the organizational pattern did not take place suddenly. Churches long accustomed to act independently, often with no regard to the needs of the larger fellowship, had to develop a new consciousness of corporate identity and purpose before radical alterations could be effected. To persons who associated complete local autonomy with Baptist orthodoxy, any move to infringe upon that autonomy was viewed with suspicion. Only as a clearer understanding of the nature and mission of the church and of principles inherent in Baptist theory and practice was developed, did resistance to major reconstruction dissolve.

1. BAPTIST ORGANIZATION IN RETROSPECT

Although we might proceed directly to a description of the present polity of the American Baptist Churches, it seems worthwhile to present a review of the historical process leading up to the present. To retrace our steps will provide a perspective in which to understand our system. We can see how Baptists in the Northern States adopted a method of cooperative work inconsistent with "the associational principle" and the problems which resulted. Also, an historical picture will reveal the continuity of fundamental Baptist concerns throughout the process, so that the present organizational pattern appears to be the product of evolutionary development and not the result of having abandoned the basic insights of our forebears.

Anticipation of National Organization

It is interesting to observe that, even as early as 1770,

while the number of churches and associations was still small, proposals were made which looked forward to the development of a national organization. A Philadelphia pastor, Morgan Edwards, suggested the outlines for such a body. Its advantages were described by him as follows: "It introduces into the visible church what are called joints and bands whereby the whole body is knit together and compacted for increase by that which every part supplieth. And therefore it is that I am so anxious to render the same combination of Baptist Churches universal upon this continent."[2]

Even earlier, another Baptist had written to James Manning, the president of Rhode Island College, in a similar vein. Written on the occasion of the founding of the Warren Association in Rhode Island, the letter stated:

For, as particular members are collected together and united in one body, which we call a particular church, to answer those ends and purposes which could not be accomplished by any single member, so a collection and union of churches into one associational body may easily be conceived capable of answering those still greater purposes which any particular church could not be equal to. And, by the same reason, a union of associations will still increase the body in weight and strength, and make it good that a three-fold cord is not easily broken.[3]

The foregoing quotations are samples of a widespread sentiment which contemplated the expansion of the associational principle embodied in the Philadelphia Baptist Association. The missionary and educational movements, however, had not yet arisen to make the churches feel the urgency of completing a national organization. By the time that the necessity did become apparent, other influences were at work which shifted the development to a new direction.

[2]Quoted by William Wright Barnes, *The Southern Baptist Convention, 1845-1953*, page 9. Nashville: Broadman Press, 1954.
[3]*Ibid.*, page 2.

Two Conflicting Plans for Organizational Development

Early in the nineteenth century a series of new movements affected the course of Baptist growth and development. A fresh awareness of the missionary and evangelistic responsibility of the church called forth new forms of cooperation among churches and among denominations. This interest, which included home and foreign missions, education, and the dissemination of Bibles and Christian literature, elicited new methods of raising funds to meet the great opportunities.

It was this rising tide of interest in missions which crystallized Baptist interest in some additional organization. When the Judsons and Luther Rice changed their denominational loyalty from Congregationalist to Baptist, there arose an urgent need for some means of supporting them as missionaries in Burma. Luther Rice returned to America to seek the support of Baptists, and in conjunction with Baptist leaders of Boston and Philadelphia he spearheaded a move to awaken the interest of the churches in organizing to support foreign missions. At about the same time there was a growing desire to extend the work of home missions and to establish educational institutions, which gave a further impetus to the development of a national organization.

At this juncture, it was not clear what forms of organization the Baptists would adopt in order to participate in these new movements. The early pattern of the Philadelphia Baptist Association offered a basis for the development of an associational life on the national level. The natural line of development would have been to expand the associations into state and national organizations, and there was strong sentiment in favor of such a plan. State and national conventions would be organized and related to the local churches through the associations. Through such an organization the Baptists could meet the challenge of missions, education, evangelism, and publications.

In opposition to the natural expansion of the associational

principle, however, were an individualistic spirit and vested local interests. Many people feared any tendency toward centralization of authority, and they favored the formation of separate voluntary societies to sponsor each particular missionary and educational concern. Such societies were not composed of churches but of assorted individuals or groups who were interested in the project represented by a given society. Membership being voluntary, it was open to persons of any or no denomination upon payment of dues. Forgetting the theology which had undergirded the associational principle, the advocates of this viewpoint wished to bypass the older design in favor of the "society method" of cooperative work. Between 1814 and 1826, there was a divided opinion, but the strong desire for an integrated denomination seemed likely to win the contest. By the latter date, however, the individualistic spirit had triumphed, and the decentralized pattern represented by the societies was adopted.

The Triennial Convention

In 1814, it was the hope of Luther Rice to see the development of a unified national body of Baptists. It was his plan to lead in the formation of a national organization made up of representatives of state conventions, and these in turn would be composed of delegates from associations and local societies. Dr. Thomas Baldwin of Boston, also envisioned a similar close-knit denominational body, as did many other ministers. There were other influential leaders, however, who wished to avoid any tendencies toward a strong ecclesiastical organization. Under the pressure of time, the leaders formed a Baptist Missionary Convention which had for its one purpose the support of foreign missions. It was expected by some that this "Triennial Convention," as it was commonly called, could be developed into a more comprehensive body later, and various attempts were made to expand and strengthen it.

The first step toward extending the purpose of the Triennial Convention came in 1817 when the constitution was amended. A need was felt for a national Baptist college to prepare ministers, and there was a desire to combine home and foreign missions in the work of this agency. By changing the constitution, power was given to the Board authorizing it "to appropriate a portion of the funds to domestic missionary purposes." The Board was also authorized, when funds should become adequate, "to institute a classical and theological seminary, for the purpose of aiding young men" of promise for the ministry. The purpose of the missionary convention was further expanded in 1820 when the name was changed to state its objectives broadly as "foreign missions and other important objects relating to the Redeemer's kingdom."

With these constitutional revisions the foundation had been established for a comprehensive denominational life, but the machinery to implement this dream was yet to be completed. Membership in the Triennial Convention was based upon the payment of a sum of money by either an individual or a local society. Therefore, it was not really a denominational body representing the churches, but rather a voluntary society composed of dues-paying members who might not even be Baptists. However, at that point in its development, the Triennial Convention was intended to be only a stopgap until a denominational organization could be effected.

State Conventions as a Necessary Link

A necessary step in the process of completing the national body was the formation of state conventions, which could be joined into a general convention. Local churches would then be represented by delegates to the association, and associations would send delegates to the state convention. The latter would in turn choose representatives to attend the General Convention. In this way the churches would be united in a nationwide denominational organization of a representative type.

The first state convention was formed in South Carolina in 1821. Favoring an integrated denominational body, those who led the movement to establish this organization framed it in a way which would coordinate Baptist work in the state. The associations were united into a state convention, and the aims stated in its constitution included missions and education. Before long, a college had been started, which was owned and controlled by the state organization. Home and foreign missions too were promoted under state auspices. It was ready to become one of the links between churches and a national convention. In the same year a similar move was taken in New York State, where a state convention was made up of delegates from associations. However, in that state the intention of its sponsors was thwarted by competing interests.

Within the next few years, similar conventions were begun in ten other states. The Massachusetts Convention, begun in 1824, anticipated the time when it would become a link between the associations and a national convention. Its constitution stated that "whenever a General Convention formed from State Conventions throughout the United States shall be formed or designed, it shall be in the power of this Convention to send delegates to meet in such Convention."[4] Editorials and articles appeared which looked forward to the culmination of the plan to transform the Triennial Convention into a representative Baptist body on a national level.

Triumph of the "Society Method"

It had been anticipated that by 1826 the dream would be realized; but before that date arrived, certain strong local interests had thwarted the whole movement. In New

[4]Quoted by W. S. Hudson, "Stumbling into Disorder," *Foundations*, April, 1958, page 47.

York the new state convention sought to bring missionary and educational interests together under the auspices of the single Baptist body. However, the educational society which controlled the new college, unwilling to relinquish this control, remained independent. Moreover, the Hamilton Missionary Society did not wish to lose its identity. Instead of merging the mission society with the State Convention, therefore, the reverse procedure took place, and the state organization became the Baptist Missionary Convention of the State of New York. Hence, instead of a truly representative Baptist convention emerging in New York, the state body became a missionary society based upon contributions of interested people.

At the meeting of the Triennial Convention in 1826, the influence of the New York State delegation, coupled with that of influential men from Boston, prevented the anticipated fulfillment of the hope for a national convention. Instead of moving toward a more unified and representative agency, the Triennial Convention voted in 1826 to restrict its interests to foreign missions, and its money basis for membership was retained. Separate societies directed the work of publication and home missions, and each educational institution was operated by independent societies. At last the decentralized pattern had won, and Baptist organization became atomistic. The same spirit which had led to the frustration of the associational principle now fostered an increasing trend toward local autonomy, which removed the idea of independence from the context of the lordship of Christ over his church. The tendencies toward independence divorced missionary and educational agencies from responsibility to the churches and hampered the development of a coherent and efficient denominational organization in the United States.

The significant decision of 1826 determined the denominational pattern of Baptists in the North, but Southern Baptists followed a different course. The Southern Baptist

Convention was constituted in 1845, after a secession of southerners from the Triennial Convention and the American Baptist Home Mission Society. Instead of employing the society method, this convention carried on its missionary activities through its own foreign and domestic mission boards. In order to enable the convention to assume responsibility for the whole range of Christian work, it was allowed by its constitution to organize other boards as they might be needed. In this way a basis was laid for the development of a more integrated denomination.

The difference between the "convention method" and the "society method" has had an important bearing upon the development of Baptist life in the North. Instead of having agencies which were integral parts of the denomination, a series of independent corporations operated by self-perpetuating boards of managers was developed. The American Baptist Foreign Mission Society, the Woman's American Baptist Foreign Mission Society, the American Baptist Home Mission Society, the Woman's American Baptist Home Mission Society, the American Baptist Education Society, the American Baptist Historical Society, and the American Baptist Publication Society were all legally incorporated institutions responsible only to a constituency determined by the payment of membership fees. Even state conventions became missionary societies of the same type. Theological seminaries and colleges were operated by independent groups through self-perpetuating boards of trustees, instead of being under control of the denomination. While there was some attempt to coordinate the work of separate agencies, there was a great deal of competition and wasteful duplication.

With the passing of years the need for a more unified denomination became clear, but the road to reorganization was blocked. The triumph of the society method had promoted a spirit of independence which was stronger than the cooperative spirit. Vested interests developed in the independent societies which were unwilling to surrender their power or prerogatives for the good of the larger work.

Moreover, the nineteenth century saw an erosion of the older theology of the church which could have provided a basis for a better structure. Under the impact of individualism and evangelicalism, the Baptists of the nineteenth century had undergone subtle changes and now came to see themselves in a new perspective. The strict Calvinism which had characterized the denomination earlier was now being dissolved, although the process was largely unconscious. By the end of the century, in place of the early bonds which had united Baptists in associations, a new interpretation of independence was in vogue which denied that there was such a thing as the "interdependence" of Baptist churches. The idea of the universal church tended to drop out of common use, and some people denied that the New Testament knew of any other meaning of "church" besides that of the local church. Oblivious of their close relationship to English Dissenters, some Baptists even began to deny that they were Protestants. Earlier adherence to confessional statements gave way to the strange idea that Baptists have no creeds or confessions except the New Testament. Furthermore, the theory that Baptist churches cannot be represented came to be accepted as a traditional Baptist view: the churches could send only "messengers" to their assemblies—not delegates.

2. NORTHERN BAPTIST CONVENTION

As the defects of a very decentralized denomination forced consideration of a better system, it was difficult to rally support for anything more than modest change. The independent "societies" and the local churches were jealous of their autonomy, and any move to interfere with it was quickly checked. In 1907, the Northern Baptist Convention was constituted to coordinate the work of the various societies, but it was an awkward compromise between "convention" and "society" methods. Instead of merging the several organizations into a single entity, the Act of Incorporation and By-Laws provided for a loose federation of societies and churches. From the outset there was continuing tension between preserving the independence of churches and societies and achieving effective, united action.

Relationship to Societies

The constituent societies were designated as *cooperating organizations*, but each one remained legally separate, and the relationship with the Convention could be terminated upon a year's notice. Unity of operation was secured by holding the annual meetings of the societies simultaneously with the Northern Baptist Convention and by allowing the delegates to the Convention to be considered voting members of the separate societies. As a coordinating agency, an Executive Committee was to include the officers of the Convention, its past presidents, and thirty other members. The prime objective of the Convention was cooperation in raising funds, and each society agreed to regulate its spending in accord with a budget prepared by a finance committee and approved by the Convention. However, even this limited purpose was often frustrated by lack of coordination among denominational agencies.

Relationship to State Conventions and City Societies

Also related to the Convention were the state conventions and city societies, which were called *affiliating organizations*. Having been conceived originally as links in the chain between local churches and a national body, the state conventions gradually extended their functions: They added new departments and activities, fostering Christian education and youth work, campus ministries, assisting churches in finding pastors, and promoting national programs.

For years there was poor correlation between state conventions, city societies, and national organizations. Although the former played an important part in shaping policies of the national agencies and in making up budgets, the roles and relationships of state and national organizations were poorly defined. Much of the interaction between these two levels rested upon custom.

Dissatisfaction with Existing System Increases

By mid-twentieth century the Northern (American) Baptist Convention had become conscious of the inadequacies of its loosely federated system, and there was growing desire for greater unity and efficiency. Having experienced theological tensions, large-scale defections, stagnation in the large cities, and a weakened evangelistic thrust, they began some serious self-examination. Their dissatisfaction with themselves was partly due to a rate of growth which compared unfavorably with that of most of the other major denominational bodies. In particular, the phenomenal growth of Southern Baptists subsequent to 1940 made the northern group of churches conscious of their own almost static membership figures. They were also concerned by the lack of a strong denominational consciousness such as that which characterized the Southern Baptists.

Although the problems of the American Baptist Convention could not be attributed to a single cause, the lack of a cohesive organization seemed to be a hindrance to concerted action. In comparing the American and Southern Baptists, one should take account of sociological factors which have made the latter more homogeneous and have contributed to the shaping of its character and program. To some extent, however, the strong cooperative spirit and denominational loyalty of the Southern Baptists have been aided by their organizational structure, although the connection between local churches and convention agencies are vague.

Many people were convinced that advantages would follow the improvement of organizational patterns, but they did not expect such changes alone to bring about renewal. Reorganization, therefore, was paralleled by a series of emphases which were intended to provide a sounder basis for denominational life. Special emphasis was placed upon Baptist history and a theology of the church. Theological conferences dealt with ecclesiology; a new journal *(Foundations: A Baptist Journal of History and Theology)* was founded; the Advisory Board for Theological Studies was established; and a new *A History of the Baptists* was written by Dr. Robert G. Torbet. Significant articles illuminating Baptist history and examining the past in the light of a biblical and theological view of the church were published. *Baptist Concepts of the Church,* edited by Professor Winthrop S. Hudson, contained studies on Baptist thought and practice regarding the church; and the first edition of the present *A Baptist Manual of Polity and Practice* was written at the request of the General Council. Thus, a conscious effort was made to involve both laypersons and clergy in serious reflection about the nature and mission of the church in the light of Scriptures and of Baptist history. These efforts contributed to the formation of a new climate of opinion, which enabled the denomination to study its structure more seriously, with a view to becoming more efficient in its mission.

3. CREATING A UNIFIED DENOMINATION: THE AMERICAN BAPTIST CHURCHES/U.S.A.

Since the formation of the Northern Baptist Convention in 1907, numerous committees have been appointed to suggest plans for improving the organization. Twice, comprehensive studies were made by outside agencies, as a result of which drastic changes were recommended. Successive modifications were made in a piecemeal fashion, and there was a continuing tension between aims expressed in the incorporating documents. On the one hand, "the independence of the local church" was to be protected; but the Convention was to "promote denominational unity and efficiency."[5] In 1950, the first General Secretary was appointed; the name was changed to the American Baptist Convention; and the General Council recommended sweeping changes. Since 1950, a steady movement toward achieving a coherent, efficient denominational organization is apparent.

Two Important Steps

Symbolic of the mood to bring national agencies into more harmonious relationships was the vote, in 1958, at Cincinnati, to move the agencies to a central headquarters at Valley Forge, Pennsylvania. The main offices of the Ministers and Missionaries Benefit Board remained in New York City, and the Historical Society with its collection of records continued to operate at Rochester; but the other societies moved to the new location.

In 1961, at Portland, Oregon, an important reorganizational step was taken. The General Council was expanded to ninety-six, more than doubling its former size. With forty-six voting members and fifty nonvoting members from the incorporated boards, the cooperating societies, and the affiliated organizations, the intention was to bring all state secretaries, the heads of other agencies, and a number of staff persons into the General Council. At the same time, members of the Council were to have representatives on all the boards and divisions. Thus, communication among various departments of denominational life would be facilitated, and those responsible for interpreting policies and programs in the states and city societies would share in making decisions. The administrative heads of the program boards became associate general secretaries of the

[5] "Act of Incorporation" for Northern Baptist Convention.

American Baptist Convention. Uniform educational standards for ordination were soon adopted, and a study was begun which was to eventuate in a more effective support system for ministers.

The SAAR Project

Continuing desire for a more rational organization led to the appointment of a Commission for the Study of Administrative Areas and Relationships (SAAR). Instructed by the General Council to study the existing patterns of administrative units, the Commission recommended that the American Baptist Convention be divided into fifteen "regions," subdivided into "areas," with a core staff of specialists and area ministers. Beginning its work in 1962, the SAAR Commission kindled interest in its plan, and the result was the formation of several regions, combining more than a single state. Several city societies were reluctant to merge with a region, and in 1977 there were still thirty-seven Regions (8), State Conventions (20), and Standard City Societies (9). (These will be referred to hereafter as R/S/C units.)

SCODS Proposal Adopted

More fundamental changes were to result from a Study Commission on Denominational Structure (SCODS), appointed in 1968 at Boston. By then a number of factors had produced greater openness to changing the organization so as to achieve more efficiency and a better balance between the independence and interdependence of local congregations. As state conventions reorganized, and as commissions considered patterns of organization, there was evident a determination to take account of theological principles as well as historic Baptist concerns as they designed a new system.

In 1969, at Seattle, "A Statement of Purpose" was adopted as a guideline for organizational proposals. The intent

to subordinate merely pragmatic considerations to fundamental theological convictions was evident in the language
of this document. Describing the American Baptist Convention as "a manifestation of the church universal," it
declared an intention to "seek such a balance of freedom
and order as will keep all parts of the Convention open to
the guidance of the Holy Spirit and at the same time enable
them to work responsibly to carry out the common task of
mission and ministry." It also expressed an intention "to
implement and not to alter the objects of the corporation
as stated in the Act of Incorporation." Thus, attention was
to be given to a biblical view of the church and to Baptist
heritage in the formulation of plans for the future. Further
expansion of biblical concepts of the church and of Baptist
tradition were set forth in a "Preamble" to the SCODS
proposals.

Extensive changes resulted from the adoption of the
SCODS plan, which was adopted at Denver in 1972. The
official name was changed from "The American Baptist
Convention" to the "American Baptist Churches in the
U.S.A." The new name signified both the churchly and the
national dimensions, and it underlined the principle that
local congregations were constituent parts of the Convention.

At the heart of the plan was the creation of a General
Board composed of representatives of all the churches,
making this Board the legislative body of the denomination
and vesting it with authority to make decisions and to
formulate policy. Thus, through elected representatives,
the churches could speak and act definitively on matters
of common concern. Provisions were made to ensure that
a proportionate number of men and women, clergy and
laypersons, ethnic groups, youth, and any other minorities
would be represented on the General Board.

It might seem that the removal of authority to make
decisions from the large annual meeting to the smaller

group was a step away from democracy. In reality, however, a more genuine representative democracy was made possible. The older method of making decisions by the vote of those attending an annual meeting had not been representative, as analyses of registration records show. At the typical Convention, only one-fourth to one-third of the churches had delegates present. In 1971, for example, 3,249 delegates were registered out of a potential 21,000. Of those attending, 70 percent were pastors and their wives, leaving the laity greatly underrepresented. Moreover, it had long been obvious that three thousand or more persons could not be a deliberative body which could carefully consider issues before voting on them.

Therefore the plan called for biennial gatherings for celebration, inspiration, information, and fellowship. Delegates would elect the officers of the ABC and representatives-at-large for the General Board. The Biennial Meeting could also express opinions of the Delegates on issues of concern, and it retained the power to make changes in Bylaws. Other decisions and policies would be decided by the General Board.

Election Districts were to be established for the purpose of choosing Representatives, members of the General Board. These were to be made up, as nearly as possible, of forty to sixty churches conveniently located for such a meeting. In 1976, there were 142 of these Election Districts. Every church was asked to send delegates to participate in the election of a representative to the General Board. In addition to the Election District representatives, one-fourth of the General Board members are members-at-large elected at the Biennial Meeting. Also, six other persons are on the Board: the President of the ABC, the Vice-President, the immediate past President, and the Executive Directors of the American Baptist Women, American Baptist Men, and Ministers' Council. Although the number of representatives can fluctuate with changes in the number of churches and members, the General Board is expected to number around 200. In 1976, the total was 195.

A further step toward unifying the national structure was a provision that the members of program boards would be chosen from the membership of the General Board, rather than by separate elections. The Board of Educational Ministries (BEM), Board of International Ministries (BIM), and the Board of National Ministries (BNM) have forty or more members, appointed from the General Board. The fourth Related Board, the Ministers and Missionaries Benefit Board (M and M) has twelve to eighteen members. The chief administrative officer of each of these Related Boards was to be an Associate General Secretary of the American Baptist Churches.

The General Secretary of the ABC/U.S.A. was invested with more authority and responsibility than had belonged to predecessors. Elected by the General Board, the term of office was to be four years, with no limitation on the number of terms one could serve. As the administrative head of the denomination, the General Secretary was to coordinate the activities of the Related Boards, to aid in personnel selection, to be in charge of ecumenical relations, and to give leadership and direction to the American Baptist Churches.

Culmination of Reorganization: SCOR

With the adoption of the SCODS plan, a national structure had been developed which made local churches constituents of a representative body. It remained unclear, however, what the relationship of the regional bodies (Regions, State Conventions, Standard City Societies) was to the national organization. Although the original instructions to the SCODS Commission had included the examination of the relationships of R/S/C units to national agencies, lack of time had prohibited completion of this stage of the process. The SCODS report, therefore, had recommended that another commission be appointed to consider this unfinished business.

Accordingly, in 1974, a Study Commission on Relationships (SCOR) was appointed by the General Board to draw up a plan by which the thirty-seven R/S/C units might be integrated into the new structure. Proposals made by SCOR were presented, in 1977, to the Biennial Meeting delegates at San Diego, who voted to approve the By-law changes to implement the SCOR recommendations. The suggested changes were a logical extension of principles embodied in SCODS, aiming to complete the process of making the American Baptist Churches an inclusive body, encompassing national, regional, and local levels.

The plan recommended that the regional bodies (R/S/Cs) become constituents of the American Baptist Churches. As such they could send representatives to the Biennial Meetings and to the General Board. This meant that the ABC would have a dual constituency—Cooperating Churches (directly represented through their representatives) and regional bodies, through their representatives. In order to maintain the size of the General Board, however, it was decided that the Election District representatives would also serve as representatives of their respective regional bodies. Regional Boards could send delegates to Election District Assemblies, so that they would have a voice in the selection of the representatives who represent both the Cooperating Churches and the Regional Boards. Representatives were expected to make a conscientious effort to become informed about the opinions of their constituencies and to make periodic reports to them, but they could not be instructed how to vote on particular issues.

An attempt was made to distinguish between the roles of regional bodies in their direct relation to churches of their respective areas and in their roles as integral parts of the national body. Each would have an Executive Minister and a Regional Board. The Regional Boards would develop programs and make policies on matters clearly related to their own territories.

In aspects of mission which could be accomplished more effectively by the denomination as a whole, however, the Regional Boards were accountable to the General Board. Executive Ministers of regional bodies were to be elected in consultation with the General Secretary of the ABC. The General Secretary could also participate in the evaluation of the Executive Ministers, who in their relationship to ABC matters were known as Regional Secretaries. The General Board could assign tasks to Regional Boards, and it could monitor and evaluate their performance of these assignments.

The Regional Secretaries serve on the General Staff Council (successor to the former National Staff Council), and they are also members of the Regional Executive Ministers Council. Through these two agencies they have a voice in policy recommendations, evaluations, and other matters of common concern to the constituents of the American Baptist Churches. Their role, however, is advisory, and the power to make decisions in most matters rests with the General Board. An important aspect of the relationship among Regional, National, and General Boards is the "Common Budget Covenant," which is binding and can be changed only with the approval of all parties.

As safeguards to the integrity of the regional bodies, there are certain checks and balances. The Regional Boards are represented directly on the General Board, and they are indirectly represented also by representatives of the Cooperating Churches. Thus, they have assurance that the concerns of their respective areas will be heard. The opportunity of the Executive Ministers (Regional Secretaries) to be on the General Staff Council and on the Regional Executive Ministers Council also offers opportunity for input from the regional bodies. In case of differences between a Regional Board and the General Board, or National

Board, procedures are established for adjudicating the point at issue.

In a few matters, there are limitations upon the authority of the General Board. Any proposal to merge with another religious body, to amend the "Statement of Purpose of the ABC," or to change the "free church" polity of the denomination is subject to ratification by two-thirds of the Regional Boards and two-thirds of the delegates in Biennial Meeting. Decisions to inaugurate capital fund-raising campaigns require ratification by two-thirds of the Regional Boards, but not of the Biennial delegates.

The national character of the denomination has been emphasized by many changes in nomenclature. There are now three sets of boards: General Board, National Boards (the Related Boards), and Regional Boards. Executive Ministers of regional bodies are also, in their relationship to the General Board, Regional Secretaries of the ABC. The administrative heads of the National Boards (formerly called Executive Secretaries and Associate General Secretaries) are now to be called "Executive Directors" of their Related Boards, and at the same time "National Secretaries of the ABC." There are also three councils: the General Staff Council, the National Executive Council (the General Secretary and the National Secretaries), and the Regional Executive Ministers Council (the General Secretary and the Executive Ministers). Other new terms are: the ABC Nominating Committee, and the Biennial ABC Program Committee.

A fundamental concept employed by SCOR as a basis for establishing and clarifying the relationships of regional bodies to national agencies is that of "covenant." Through a common "Covenant of Relationships" among the General, National, and Regional Boards the former "Affiliated Organizations" were to become "Covenanting Regional Boards." The covenant contains biblical, theological, and operational assumptions and plans for ratifying and amending the document. Accompanying "Statements of Agreement" contain an understanding of initial responsibilities and programmatic matters, as well as procedures for adjudicating differences which might arise between General and Regional Boards.

There was some dissent to the SCOR proposals at the San Diego Biennial Meeting, but it was surprisingly small. A number of amendments to proposed By-law changes were suggested, most of which were intended to help retain a larger measure of autonomy in the regional bodies. After debating a few of the amendments and voting on them, it was apparent that the overwhelming majority of delegates favored the trend toward integrating the regional bodies into the structure which had been set in motion following approval of the SCODS recommendations. Such an outcome would have been unthinkable ten or fifteen years earlier, but the growing concern for denominational unity and cohesiveness had shifted loyalties away from local autonomy toward arrangements for a more unified denomination.

Only one step remained after the approval of the delegates in 1977. Before the changes could become finally effective, two-thirds of the R/S/C units would have to adopt the new system. On January 1, following such ratification, the plan would go into effect, provided that adoption be completed not later than October 1, 1978. None of the "Affiliating Organizations" is compelled to become a "Covenanting Organization." It is possible to remain in the status of Affiliating Organization, although some limitations would be placed upon voting rights in the General Staff Council. By 1981, there will be a review of the situation.

At last, many converging influences had wrought a change in the consciousness of American Baptists and produced a radically different structure from the old, poorly defined Northern Baptist Convention. Its success, however, requires the active interest and participation of the churches in electing representatives, keeping informed about issues and programs, and working in a cooperative spirit with Regional, National, and General Boards. Like any democracy, the American Baptist Churches could become a centralized bureaucratic structure by the failure of church members to become involved. At the same time, it offers tremendous opportunities for more effective cooperation in renewing life in the churches and making an impact upon society.

4. RELATIONSHIP TO DENOMINATIONAL SCHOOLS

While integration of regional, national, and local levels had been effected, and a multiplicity of functions was incorporated in appropriate national boards, one area of relationship remained unresolved, viz., that of denominational schools. Numerous colleges and theological seminaries had been established over the years, and they were recognized by the Board of Educational Ministries and its predecessors. Receiving virtually no direct financial support from any denominational agency, and poorly supported by churches, the schools became very independent. One by one, many colleges severed ties with the denomination, and seminaries were not subject to controls from either state or national denominational organizations.

A denomination can derive a great deal of cohesive power from its schools, but only when strong mutual bonds exist between them. The schools need to be undergirded by adequate support, and at the same time they should be accountable to the churches which support them. In the Southern Baptist Convention, the North American Baptist General Conference, and the Baptist General Conference of America, colleges and seminaries have mutual obligations and both parties benefit from the relationships. Efforts to establish closer ties between schools and the denomination in the Northern Baptist Convention and its successors have not been very effective. Although a plan to adapt "covenants" between each school and the ABC was adopted in 1977, mutual responsibilities remained tenuous. No satisfactory means of providing funds has been found, and schools have jealously guarded their independence from any attempts to influence their freedom to act.

XI

Ecumenical Relationships

Up to this point, we have been largely concerned with the relationship of Baptists to their fellow-Baptists. Few Baptists, however, would contend that such a treatment is adequate for interpreting their part in the church of Jesus Christ in these closing decades of the twentieth century. The everyday lives of pastors and churches today continually involve contacts with those of other denominations. Through their response to councils of churches, union services, evangelistic crusades, and other activities, Baptists again and again are determining the extent to which they will (or will not) become involved in interdenominational activities. Let us now consider the great movements in the Christian world which are providing the context in which these involvements are taking place.

1. THE MODERN ECUMENICAL MOVEMENT

The twentieth century has witnessed a surge of interest in Christian unity, and this trend is commonly designated "the ecumenical movement." By some people this movement has been hailed as "the great new fact of our era," while by others it has been viewed with suspicion. Probably the majority of those at the grass-roots level of the church, however, have had only a hazy notion of what is meant by the term "ecumenical,"

189

and their attitude toward the movement has been largely one of indifference.

The Term "Ecumenical"

It is hard to see how Christians in the twentieth century could be hostile or indifferent to a movement of such great significance. In great measure both of these attitudes are due to a lack of information or to misinformation which is deliberately spread by interested parties. The word "ecumenical" means essentially "world-wide," but it also signifies "oneness." Therefore the ecumenical movement indicates an emphasis upon the unity of the Christian church and the need to find ways in which that unity may be expressed in ministering to the world. It does not refer to any one particular organization, but to a spirit or a movement embodied in several organizational forms. Among the most important of these are the World Council of Churches, the National Council of Churches of Christ in the United States of America, and many state and local councils.

On scriptural grounds one could hardly object to any plans by which Christian unity might be made more visible and differences might be harmonized. For the essential idea of the church in the New Testament is a body of people united with Jesus Christ as its head. Although the word "church" is most often used in the New Testament in connection with local congregations, yet there is always implied the larger idea of "the people of God." The local group represents the total church of God in a particular place, but it is only part of the total Christian community. Jesus Christ prayed that his followers in generations to come might "become perfectly one" (John 17:23). Paul urged the Ephesians to maintain the unity of the Spirit, reminding them that "there is one body and one Spirit . . . one Lord, one faith, one baptism, one God and Father of us all" (Eph. 4:4-6). We have become so accustomed to seeing divisions within the church that we are apt to take the present situation as normal. It is highly doubtful that the writers of the New Testament would have considered it so, for they assumed a fundamental unity of the church.

Nor could anyone oppose an ecumenical emphasis upon the grounds of Baptist history, for the early Baptists were not sectarian. Their statement of faith affirmed that "there is one holy, catholic church." The attitude of General Baptists was reflected in their "Orthodox Creed" of 1678, the subtitle of which indicated that it was "an essay to unite and confirm all true Protestants." A nonsectarian spirit also characterized the Particular Baptists, as is shown by their major doctrinal statement. Desiring to express their closeness to others, they adopted the Westminster Confession, which with a few alterations had also been used as the confessional statement of the Congregationalists. The Baptists then made a few changes with regard to their doctrines of the church, baptism, the ministry, and the relationship of the civil government to religious matters. They deliberately chose to use this Presbyterian-Congregationalist document, in order to declare their "hearty agreement with them, in that wholesome Protestant doctrine, which, with so clear evidence of Scriptures they have asserted."[1]

Anyone familiar with the writings of Baptists in the seventeenth and eighteenth centuries will realize that they were not sectarians; they did not believe themselves to have exclusive right to be called the church. They frequently asserted their identity as Protestants, and recognized that their fundamental convictions were shared by others. They felt particularly close to Presbyterians and Congregationalists, but as John Smyth's party had stated in 1612: "All penitent and faithful Christians are brethren in the communion of the outward church, wheresoever they live, by what name soever they are known."[2] In America there were many occasions where Baptists co-operated with other denominations in missions to the Indians, Bible societies, and other matters. Baptists believed that they had

[1] Lumpkin, *op. cit.*, page 245.
[2] *Ibid.*, page 137.

certain convictions to preserve, but they did not pretend to have a monopoly on Christian truth.

The Theory of Denominationalism

The word "denomination" came to be applied to the diverse groups of Protestants in the eighteenth century. Baptists have referred to themselves as a denomination, implying that they considered themselves but a part of a larger body. "Denomination" means simply "called by a name," and the assumption underlying the theory of denominationalism is that there is a greater unity which binds all of the diverse groups called by different names into one entity. It recognizes that there are many differences in outward forms, in worship ceremonies, and even in doctrinal formulations, but that there is a basic unity in the acknowledgement of the lordship of Christ over his church.

To accept the term "denomination" presupposes several things. In the first place, it recognizes that in this world it is impossible for men to see eye-to-eye on everything. Brought up under different circumstances, conditioned by different experiences, men are bound to arrive at different opinions. Under the pressure of environmental circumstances, there will be different external forms of worship and practice. To accept the inevitability of such differences does not lead to a conclusion that differences are unimportant, but it simply accepts realistically the fact that there will be such variety. Because it is important to reach the truth as fully as possible, those who have different perspectives and opinions must come together to engage in dialogue with each other. Under the leading of the Spirit, it is to be hoped that there may be a meeting of minds, and that a fuller apprehension of the truth may be reached. Through conference, study, and prayer, the light of God's truth may break more fully upon men's minds. In the meantime, Christians must acknowledge each other as brethren, and work and pray together.

Secondly, to accept the theory of denominationalism outlined above is to acknowledge that Christian fellowship is founded upon something more than agreement in doctrine. Theology is important, and Christianity does involve doctrines of God, Christ, man, sin, and salvation. However, our doctrinal formulations are affected by our experiences of God's revelation, and within certain limits there is room for differing viewpoints. Therefore, the basis of fellowship must not be simply an assent to a set of propositions. Fellowship has a deeper source also than a common set of values, for it is more than an ethical system. The Christian faith at its heart involves new relationships with God and with other people, and that which binds us together is a common experience of God's grace. It involves a work of the Holy Spirit in our lives by which we become new creatures in Christ and "members one of another," as by faith we accept God's gracious offer of reconciliation and power. With all who claim such an experience and who confess Jesus Christ as Savior and Lord we are bound to work and pray together as brothers, notwithstanding differences which may exist among us.

Sometimes the unity which Christians have in Christ has been obscured by magnifying institutional differences. Forgetting the true basis of fellowship, members of different denominational groups become so isolated from one another that they seem to lack any real unity. The consequence is that the world has often been more impressed by the divisions within the church than by our underlying oneness. Surely some visible expression ought to be given to the unity which we have, so that the body of Christ may not appear to be divided and at war within itself.

The practical question, however, is, What form should such visible unity take? Should we seek to merge all Christians into a single Protestant body? Or, is it enough to form federations which provide a meeting place for representatives of the denominations to gather and channels through which they can co-operate? There is no unanimity of opinion among Christians as to the way in which we should seek to give expression to our unity. Whether we shall ever bring all Christians under a single organizational roof is doubtful, and it is questionable whether such an outcome would be desirable. Perhaps the merging of all denominations within a given nation or locality into one church is desirable, but there are some advantages to having some different denominations. If all Protestants were united in a single organization, we might easily become less self-critical. The existence of denominations serves as a check to the pretenses of one another, reminding us that all human institutions are fallible and stand under the judgment of God.

To concede that there may be a place for denominations, however, should not lead to complacency about divisions which have no real reason for their existence. When our divisions rest upon barriers of race and color, social class and level of income, or other sociological factors, then they become reflections of the world instead of the church. Within the Christian community it is the will of Christ to break down artificial barriers between men.

On the other hand, when there are genuine insights which seem to be neglected by others, it may be necessary for a denomination to keep alive that particular emphasis. Practical considerations of language and geography may also provide justification for denominational existence, but these should not be perpetuated longer than they are needed.

In short, we of the Christian church have more denominational bodies today than are really warranted, but not so many meaningless divisions as many of our critics would imply.

The Modern Ecumenical Movement

There is today an increasing concern on the part of churches to find more ways in which to give visible expression to Christian unity. The "ecumenical movement" is the phrase used to describe efforts to attain such unity. Although there has been much complacency about our divisions in the past, it would be a mistake to think that the desire for the unity of the church is something quite new. Actually, there had been one church in western Europe for centuries prior to the Reformation; and when the Reformation churches became separated from that church, there was deep distress on the part of leading Reformers. Martin Luther, John Calvin, and others sought ways of promoting reunion among Protestants and with the Roman Catholic Church, because unity was important to them. In every century since that time, there have been movements toward greater church unity, but the sense of need for such unity seems to be greater today than ever before.

What are the reasons for the renewed emphasis upon Christian unity? To some extent outward pressures have made the need for co-operation and fellowship more apparent. The threats of imperialistic Communism and the fear of another world war more terrible than any previous one have certainly been factors which have challenged the church. In the United States, the expansion of the Roman Catholic Church and its ability to influence government and media of communication have made Protestants more aware of their own weakness and division. More positive influences than these have also been at work. For one thing, the renewal of biblical studies in this generation has led to a clearer conception of the importance of the church in the purpose of God. With a deeper appreciation of the nature and mission of the church, the seriousness of division has become more obvious. Moreover, the concern for evangelism and missions has made it imperative to present a more united witness to the world. Increasing secularism in the West and the confusion caused by divisions on mission fields has emphasized the need for a more persuasive witness.

Indeed, it was on the mission fields that the need for unity and co-operation was felt most intensely. Here the ecumenical movement may be said to have been born. Early in the missionary experience of William Carey, the Baptist founder of the modern missionary movement, the need for Christian co-operation has become plain. In 1806, he proposed that a "general association of all denominations of Christians from the four quarters of the world" be held every ten years. Although his suggestion was not taken up at the time, the need for such meetings became more pressing. During the years after 1850, more and more regional missionary conferences were held. Co-operation was developed along several lines, such as joint translation projects, co-operative efforts in printing, sponsorship of hospitals and schools, and comity agreements to prevent wasted effort through overlapping of fields.

It was in 1910 that a very significant missionary conference was held at Edinburgh, Scotland. Here, 1355 delegates representing missionary societies from all over the world met. They sought to discover by consultation how the churches could help, instead of hampering or competing with, one another, to pool whatever knowledge and experience each had gained. Out of this conference emerged three new movements which paved the way for the forming of the World Council of Churches.

The first was the International Missionary Council, formed in 1921 in order to achieve a greater measure of practical co-operation among missionaries. Besides providing a small, permanent organization to carry on its work continuously, it has held four great world conferences—at Jerusalem, in 1928; at Tambaram, India, in 1938; at Whitby, Canada, in 1947; and at Willingen, Germany, in 1952. A second movement developing from the 1910 meeting was the Faith and Order Movement. One of the purposes of this was to explore together the reasons why denominations differed from each other, when they worshiped the same Lord and used the same Bible. Faith and Order held world conferences at Lausanne, Switzerland, in 1927 and at Edinburgh, Scotland, in 1937. The third great movement stemming from 1910 was the Life and Work Movement, which had a world gathering at Stockholm in 1925 and one at Oxford in 1937. Its purpose was to make possible co-operative undertakings other than missions.

It was quite natural that these three movements, with different emphases, but having many of the same people interested in each, should think of joining forces. Out of the meetings at Oxford and Edinburgh in the summer of 1937, there came a proposal to form a World Council of Churches through the merging of the Faith and Order and the Life and Work movements. Although the International Missionary Council continued its separate existence for more than two decades, it was fully co-operative with the World Council of Churches and became a division of the larger body in 1961.

2. ECUMENICAL ORGANIZATIONS

The World Council of Churches

Although necessary plans for organization of the World Council of Churches had been completed by 1939, the coming of World War II prevented their implementation. It was in 1948, at Amsterdam, that this organization finally came into being. The constitution began with a statement which describes the nature and basis of this council. It states: "The World Council of Churches is a fellowship of churches which accept our Lord Jesus Christ as God and Saviour." There are many who criticized this statement as inadequate. It was certainly inadequate for a full statement of doctrine, but it offered a minimal statement of the basis for fellowship and co-operative work. At the third General Assembly in 1961, a revised statement was adopted: "The World Council of Churches is a fellowship of churches which confess the Lord Jesus Christ as God and Saviour, according to the Scriptures, and therefore seek to fulfill their common calling to the glory of the one God, Father, Son and Holy Spirit." Assuming a great deal that is not said, it sums up the essential elements of the Christian faith by its affirmation regarding Scriptures, the triune God, and Jesus Christ. Each term is filled with implications, and the statement says a great deal in a few words.

Several useful purposes are served by the World Council of Churches. Carrying on the work of the earlier movements, it promotes biblical and theological study by interdenominational committees, and facilitates common undertakings. Through various means it seeks to encourage the development of an ecumenical spirit. As men and women from various backgrounds are brought together in study groups or for meetings on various matters, they become more aware of their kinship in Christ. Valuable books and pamphlets have been published through commissions of the council, and mutual understanding among Christian communions has been fostered. Listed among their objectives is also: "To support the churches in their task of evangelism."

The work of the World Council is carried on through (1) an assembly made up of delegates from all member churches and (2) a central committee of about ninety members which meets each year. There are also several special commissions and committees which have permanent staff members, enabling the work to be prosecuted without loss of continuity. Special committees also sponsor theological studies, keep abreast of international affairs and encourage an informed Christian conscience at points of tension, provide aid to refugees and furnish a channel through which churches may give relief to distressed areas, help interested young people find opportunities for ecumenical education abroad, and stimulate interest in evangelism and numerous other practical matters.

Some of the projects in which the agencies of the World Council have taken a part are the relocation of refugees, ministry to prisoners-of-war, relief work, and emergency aid around the world to those hit by floods, earthquakes, and other disasters. In cases where religious persecution has occurred, the World Council has sometimes been able to speak in a helpful way. When four Baptist pastors were tried in Czechoslovakia, the Baptist World Alliance was looked upon with suspicion by the governments concerned, but the World Council was able to take action.

It is sometimes claimed that the World Council of Churches is seeking to bring about a great super-church. Although some individuals doubtless desire such an outcome, a majority is definitely opposed to such an aim. The official report of the first Assembly said, "The Council disavows any thought of becoming a single unified church structure." The World Council seeks to cultivate a deeper sense of Christian unity, to make it possible to co-operate in many areas where a single denomination could not effectively operate, and to encourage Christians to fulfill their mission under God more faithfully. Feeling deeply the need for our unity to become visible, the council tries to be an agency through which that unity can be expressed. It is not always easy to forget differences, and there are many forces including misunderstanding and ignorance which work against this co-operative work. However, there is a determination to overcome obstacles for Christ's sake. As the Message of the first Assembly said: "Here at Amsterdam we have committed ourselves afresh to Him, and have covenanted with one another in constituting this World Council of Churches. We intend to stay together."

The National Council of Churches

In addition to the World Council of Churches for co-operation on a worldwide scope, there are agencies particularly devoted for co-operative Christian work on national and regional levels. For Americans, the chief means through which interdenominational Protestantism can be expressed is the National Council of the Churches of Christ in the United States of America. Organized in 1950, it was the heir of a number of earlier movements, particularly the Federal Council of Churches. In the face of complex problems, a growing Protestantism had previously sought new ways of co-operating in evangelism, missions, and Christian education in the latter part of the nineteenth century. Among these earlier interdenominational organizations were the Y.M.C.A., the Y.W.C.A., the International Society of Christian Endeavor, the Evangelical Alliance, the Uniform Lesson plan, the World's Student Christian Federation, and various others. In 1908 the Federal Council of Churches was constituted and became the main channel for co-operative work. At the same time there were other separate agencies in which Protestants co-operated for special purposes, such as the Foreign Missions Council of North America, the Home Missions Council of North America, the International Council of Religious Education, the Missionary Education Movement of the U.S. and Canada, the National Protestant Council of Higher Education, and the United Stewardship Council.

In 1950, the Federal Council and most of the special-purpose organizations were merged into the National Council of the Churches of Christ in the United States of America. The preamble states the basis of the new organization as follows: "In the Providence of God, the time has come when it seems fitting more fully to manifest oneness in Jesus Christ as Divine Lord and Savior, by the creation of an inclusive cooperative agency of the Christian churches of the United States of America to continue and extend the following general agencies of the churches and to combine all their interests and functions." Its purpose is much like that of the World Council of Churches, but carried out on a different level. In continuing the work of the Foreign Missions Council and the Home Missions Council, it provides a useful means of exchanging information and co-ordinating activities of the many denominations. Through a commission it calls together representatives of the churches to plan the Uniform Lessons for Sunday church schools. Many practical interests are served through the channels afforded by the agencies of this interdenominational organization. Although there is no integral connection between the N.C.C.C. and the W.C.C., one of the purposes of the former is "to maintain fellowship and co-operation with the World Council of Churches and with other international Christian organizations." At the same time it maintains close working relationships with the many local councils of churches over the United States and Canada, as well as with similar councils of churches in other countries.

While there may be actions of the N.C.C.C. which are open to criticism, the council itself is of such obvious value that it deserves the full support of Baptists. With the large number of denominations existing in the United States, there is bound to be duplication of effort and sometimes rivalries which are inimical to the cause of Christ. The council helps to reduce these unfortunate factors. At many points, it can provide channels of co-operation and communication, and make it possible for certain tasks to be done together which would not be done at all without such co-operation. The very nature of the church as one under Christ demands that where the branches of the church can work together they should do so.

State Councils of Churches

Many of the ecumenical concerns of the various denominations can better be expressed through state-wide co-operation than through the National or World Council. Therefore there is a significant need for the various state councils of churches, most of which have a longer history than either of the larger bodies. As a rule, state council memberships are comprised of two classes of Christian organizations operating in the state, (1) local councils of churches and (2) denominational bodies.

Typical of the work of a state council are activities such as the following: Legislative seminars and action at the state capital; ministry to migrant workers; chaplaincy at state mental, penal, and welfare institutions; special emphasis on the rural ministry within the state; programs of Christian education which can best be conducted on a broader basis than the local council or specific denomination (such as weekday religious education); and state-wide meetings by such council-related groups as United Church Women and United Church Men.

Local Councils of Churches

The point at which most churches feel closest to the ecumenical movement is the city or county council of churches. It is here that the individual Baptist can find fellowship with persons of other denominations as all work together on projects of local interest which cut across denominational lines.

Practical matters such as leadership training schools, united stewardship or canvass programs, community religious census efforts, effective use of radio and television facilities, and area-wide evangelistic crusades are natural concerns of a local council. In addition, it may sponsor United Christian Youth rallies, and may help to co-ordinate the work of United Church Women or United Church Men. Special events, such as a Reformation Sunday preaching service, a choir festival in the spring, or a training session for vacation church school workers, also help to meet a need in the community for united witness and work in Christ's behalf which it would be difficult if not impossible to accomplish in any other way.

Baptist Relationships to Ecumenical Bodies

The American Baptist and two National Baptist conventions are members of both the National and World Councils. In England, the Baptists are members likewise of both the British Council of Churches and the World Council. Because sizable minorities are opposed to such participation, American Baptists do not support these movements by contributions from the regular funds of the denomination. Gifts can be made only out of money designated specifically for that purpose. Since 1960, when certain American Baptist churches raised objections against the N.C.C.C., any church wishing to register dissent against co-operation with that body may have its name so listed in the published *Annual*.

Unlike the other major Baptist conventions, Southern Baptists are not affiliated with either of these organizations. They did co-operate in the Home Missions Council and the Foreign Missions Conference of North America for many years. They severed ties after 1950 when these organizations merged with the National Council of the Churches of Christ. Although a substantial minority favors a co-operative relationship with these larger fellowships, there is strong official disapproval of such connections. Nevertheless, some of the work of National Council agencies is of such utility that some Southern Baptists participate in them as unofficial observers and through personal contributions.

With regard to state and local councils, there is some difference in attitude. In general Baptists co-operate more freely in these than in the National or World Council. Probably the reason for this condition is that the need for co-operative efforts is more evident on this level. Through such means they can co-operate in providing new churches for growing communities, and can better attack the problems of the inner city where Protestants have been losing ground. Through councils of churches they have taken part in inter-denominational evangelistic efforts, and have united in supporting or opposing legislation pertaining to questions of religious and moral significance. Such problems as juvenile delinquency, racial tensions, and the sale of obscene literature are also dealt with more effectively by a united Christian witness than by individual churches or denominations.

3. AGENCIES FOR BAPTIST CO-OPERATION

In addition to agencies for interdenominational co-operation, there are also channels through which various Baptist groups work together. In the United States are at least twenty-seven different Baptist denominational bodies. The largest of these are the Southern Baptist Convention, the National Baptist Convention, U.S.A., Inc., the National Baptist Convention of America, and the American Baptist Convention. The other twenty-three are smaller, varying in membership from about 250,000 to as few as 50. There are also numerous Baptist groups in other countries around the world. In order to help maintain some sense of their common identity, to assist one another, and to co-operate in some mutual tasks, there are various agencies through which they work.

The Baptist World Alliance

Baptist people in all parts of the Christian world are united under the banner of the Baptist World Alliance. Organized in 1905 in London, it has met ten times at irregular intervals. Its purpose is stated in the preamble to the constitution of the Alliance: "The Baptist World Alliance, extending over every part of the world, exists in order more fully to show the essential oneness of Baptist people in the Lord Jesus Christ, to impart inspiration to the brotherhood, and to promote the spirit of fellowship, service and co-operation among its members; but this Alliance may in no way interfere with the independence of the churches or assume the administrative functions of existing organizations." In its purpose of imparting inspiration through the infrequent meetings, and in affording links by which the sense of fellowship between Baptists can be strengthened, the Alliance has been most useful. At some points it has helped to safeguard and promote full religious liberty in places around the world where such liberty has been denied or threatened. With a minimum staff of permanent workers, it cannot accomplish much beyond these things. However, it is of value for these contributions. [3]

Other Co-operative Agencies

There are other Baptist agencies through which certain activities can be co-ordinated. In the United States, the most important organization is probably the Baptist Joint Committee on Public Affairs. Most Baptist bodies in this country are members of this enterprise, which is administered through a small permanent staff located in Washington, D. C. Through a periodical called *Report from the Capital,* it disseminates information concerning laws which have been introduced or passed which have some bearing upon religious matters. Its major concern is to note points at which the cherished Baptist view of religious liberty and the constitutional guarantee of separation of church and state seem to be threatened.

In 1959, a co-operative venture in evangelism was launched by the Baptists of North America. Called the Baptist Jubilee

[3] For a history of the Baptist World Alliance, see F. Townley Lord, *Baptist World Fellowship.* Nashville: Broadman Press, 1955.

Advance, it aimed at a five-year emphasis upon evangelism, and looked forward to a joint meeting of the co-operating conventions in 1964. The co-operation in this venture was limited largely to simultaneous emphases upon evangelism; for each group carried out its own program, and methods differed greatly. Indeed, enthusiasm for co-operation between Southern Baptist Convention and American Baptist Convention in this undertaking was somewhat dampened by the fact that Southern Baptists were at the same time establishing churches in all of the states, sometimes acting competitively in a manner which ignored the presence of other Baptists in a given area.

Need for Further Co-operation

There is need for greater co-operation and co-ordination of work among Baptists in America, but the individualism of Baptists has opposed the development of better integration of activities. Since there are no longer any territorial limits recognized by either Southern or American Baptists, some means of achieving closer co-operation between the two bodies should be effected. While there were geographical boundaries within which each worked, there was some justification for continuing as separate conventions. Since all comity agreements have been repudiated and both have churches in the same territories, and sometimes within the same communities, unfortunate competition is inevitable even with the best of intentions. Moreover, the nature of Christian unity and practical reasons suggest some mutual benefits which would come with closer co-operation, and perhaps mergers, between Negro and predominantly white conventions.

The four largest Baptist conventions are already large and unwieldy, and the continuing expansion of Southern Baptists makes theirs increasingly so. Annual assemblies are too large for anything but inspiration and the dissemination of information, and no plan has been developed for representative meetings where decisions can be made. This condition leaves policy-making completely in the hands of executive groups with inadequately-defined authority. Merging any of the major Baptist bodies would, therefore, make them even more unmanageable than they are at present.

If a representative system of government could be adopted, however, there would be a possibility of having both efficiency and responsible church government. Such a merging of Baptists is unlikely in the foreseeable future, but it may come eventually. For the present the most realistic hope of working toward greater understanding and co-operation lies in the North American Baptist Fellowship, which was established in 1966 by several Baptist groups in Canada, Mexico, and the United States. Through such an organization, Baptists could study their common objectives and examine the meaning of Baptist identity. They could work together in common tasks, lending aid to one another and seeking to mitigate points of tension and competition. For the various Baptist conventions to continue the present trend toward occupying the same geographical areas, yet remaining in virtual isolation from each other, would be a tacit denial of the importance of the name BAPTIST.

The forces at work in the world today in opposition to the Christian church are formidable. A fragmented Christian witness will be impotent to cope with secularizing tendencies or to win back lost segments of the population to Jesus Christ. Once more we must hear with seriousness the question, "Is Christ divided?" and answer it with a resounding NO! That answer must come not only in words, but in deeds which demonstrate the unity of Christians of all denominations through worshiping and witnessing together.

Appendix I

Some Significant Dates in Baptist History

1609 The first General Baptist Church formed by English refugees in Holland, under leadership of John Smyth

1612 The first General Baptist Church on English soil, led by Thomas Helwys and John Murton

1612 Plea for freedom of worship published by Helwys; the first claim for complete religious freedom in the English language

1638 The first Particular Baptist Church begun in England

1639 Baptist beginnings in America; congregation gathered by Roger Williams

1641 Practice of immersion became more general among Baptists in England

1650 Beginning of development of formal associations among Baptists. Rapid growth of Baptists during Commonwealth period

1670 A General Association of Six-Principle Baptists formed in America

1671 Beginnings of Seventh Day Baptists in America, at Newport, Rhode Island

1677 Particular Baptists adopted revision of Westminster Confession

1678 General Baptists adopted new Confession (the "Orthodox Creed")

1689 Particular Baptists of England and Wales organized General Assembly

1707 The Particular Baptists in America formed Philadelphia Baptist Association

1750-1790 Impetus to Baptist growth in America: particularly in New England and South by successive "awakenings"

1764 Establishment of the College of Rhode Island (Brown University)

1767-1786 Struggle for religious liberty, particularly in Massachusetts and Virginia

1780 Freewill Baptists organized in New England

1792 Baptist Missionary Society founded in England; sent William Carey to India; inspired similar movements by others

1812 Adoniram Judson sails for India and Burma

1814 American Baptists form Triennial Convention for foreign missions

1817 Purpose of Triennial Convention expanded to include home missions and education, with first theological seminary begun by Baptists established in Philadelphia (transferred to Washington in 1821)

1818 Literary and Theological Institutes in Maine and New York (Colby College and Colgate Theological Seminary)

1824 Baptist General Tract Society established (forerunner of the American Baptist Publication Society)

1825 Newton Theological Institution organized

1832 American Baptist Home Mission Society organized

1832 Anti-missionary movement among Baptists (Primitive Baptists) begins to crystallize

1833 New Hampshire Confession of Faith drafted

1835 J. G. Oncken appointed by Triennial Convention as agent in Germany; marks beginning of present-day Baptists in northern Europe

1837 American Baptists founded the American and Foreign Bible Society

1845 The Southern Baptist Convention formed; marked break between Baptists of North and South in missionary undertakings

1859 Southern Baptist Theological Seminary founded at Greenville, S.C.

1870 Resolution of the Southern Baptist Convention to oppose efforts to unite Boards of North and South

1871 Organization of Woman's Baptist Foreign Mission Societies (East and West); marks more active role of women in denominational life

1877 Formation of Woman's Baptist Home Mission Societies

1882 First Session of the Baptist Congress, a forum which brought together leading Baptist pastors and teachers, North and South, to discuss theological and social issues

1894 Fortress Monroe (Va.) Conference: agreement between Baptists of North and South recognizing territorial limits; eased tensions caused by work of A.B.P.S. and A.B.H.M.S. in South

1895 Organization of the National Baptist Convention of America, the first national organization of the Negro Baptists, who had grown rapidly subsequent to their emancipation from slavery

1905 Baptist World Alliance held first meeting in London: an agency to provide fellowship among Baptists of the world

1907 Formation of the American (Northern) Baptist Convention; attempt to integrate work of various special-purpose societies

1911 Freewill Baptists merged with American (Northern) Baptist Convention

1919 The New World Movement, a five-year plan, launched by American (Northern) Baptist Convention

1925 High-water mark of the Fundamentalist-Modernist controversy of the 1920's

1943 Organization of the Conservative Baptist Foreign Mission Society; beginning of steps which led to the secession from the Northern Baptist Convention in 1947

1943 Southern Baptist Convention received some California churches into its membership; marked beginning of breakdown of comity agreements and expansion of Southern Baptists into all of the United States

1944 Founding of the American Baptist Assembly at Green Lake, Wis.

1945 World Mission Crusade launched by American (Northern) Baptists; similar move by Southern Baptists

1948 American (Northern) Baptist Convention became constituent member of the World Council of Churches; first Assembly held at Amsterdam

1950 Northern Baptists changed name to American Baptist Convention. Council on Christian Social Progress organized

1954 American Baptist Convention started campaign to raise money for Churches for New Frontiers. First Theological Conference at Green Lake initiated a series of movements reflecting and strengthening theological consensus and healing of old tensions

1957 American Baptists voted approval of CHEC (Christian Higher Education Challenge) program to raise $7,500,000

1959 The Baptist Jubilee Advance launched; five-year simultaneous effort of Baptist bodies to emphasize evangelism

1960 Ground-breaking for new national offices of American Baptist Convention at Valley Forge, Pa.

1961 Reorganization Plan adopted by the American Baptist Convention (making the convention a more coherent and efficient denominational body)

1962 National offices of American Baptist Convention at Valley Forge occupied by the agencies of the denomination

1966 Forming of the North American Baptist Fellowship

1966 A Commission on Christian Unity established by the General Council of the American Baptist Convention

1968 In response to "demands" of a Black Caucus, the General Council of the A.B.C. provided for fuller participation in denominational leadership

1970 The American Baptist Convention and the Progressive National Baptist Convention entered into an "associated relationship"

1972 Implementation of recommendations of a Study Commission on Denominational Structure: General Council replaced by a more-representative 200-member General Board, the office of the General Secretary strengthened, and name changed to "American Baptist Churches in the U.S.A."

1972 The American Baptist Churches and the Progressive National Baptist Convention agree to conduct "A Fund of Renewal" to raise $7.5 million to assist minority groups

1973 Most Baptist bodies in North America participate in KEY '73, a nationwide evangelistic effort

1977   Adoption of recommendations of the Study Commission On Relationships, at San Diego Biennial of the A.B.C./ U.S.A., calling for Covenants of Relationship between Congregational units and corporate structures of the denomination; new By-laws embodying these provisions became operative Jan. 1, 1979 after ratification by 2/3 of affiliating organizations

1979   Recommendations of a two-year Study on Women in Ministry, commissioned by the Ministers' Council in 1977, were approved by the Council

Appendix II

Church Covenants

From the earliest period of Baptist history, it has been customary for churches to adopt convenants (see *supra,* pp. 72-73). The content of such covenants has varied from time to time and place to place. Some churches have preferred to limit the statement to a general Christian commitment to Christ and his church, while others have included more specific obligations. In any case, it would seem that only such matters as have universal validity for Christians ought to be included.

Three types of church covenant are printed below. One of them is an older and more general type of covenant, and the second is one in common use among Baptist churches today. The third was adopted in 1965 by the Drexel Hill (Pa.) Baptist Church.

TYPE OF CHURCH COVENANT: A

Minister: It being made manifest by God's Word that God is pleased to walk in a way of covenant with his people, he promising to be their God and they promising to be his people;

People: We, therefore, desiring to worship and serve him, and believing it to be our duty to walk together as one body in Christ, do freely and solemnly covenant with God and with one another, and do bind ourselves in the presence of God, to acknowledge God to be our God and ourselves his people; to cleave unto the Lord Jesus, the great head of the church, as our only king and lawgiver; and to walk together in brotherly love, the Spirit of God assisting us, in all God's ways and ordinances as they have been made known or shall be made known unto us from his holy Word; praying that the God of peace, who brought from the dead our Lord Jesus, may prepare and strengthen us for every good work, working in us that which is well pleasing in his sight, through Jesus Christ our Lord, to whom be glory for ever and ever. Amen.

TYPE OF CHURCH COVENANT: B

Having been led, as we believe, by the Spirit of God, to receive the Lord Jesus Christ as our Savior, and on the profession of our faith, having been baptized in the name of the Father, and of the Son, and of the Holy Spirit, we do now in the presence of God and this assembly, most solemnly and joyfully enter into covenant with one another, as one body in Christ.

We engage, therefore, by the aid of the Holy Spirit, to walk together in Christian love, to strive for the advancement of this church in knowledge, holiness, and comfort; to promote its prosperity and spirituality; to sustain its worship, ordinances, discipline, and doctrines, to contribute cheerfully and regularly to the support of the ministry, the expenses of the church, the relief of the poor, and the spread of the gospel throughout all nations.

We also engage to maintain as far as possible family and secret devotion; to teach our children the Christian truths; to seek the salvation of our kindred and acquaintances; to walk circumspectly in the world; to be just in our dealings, faithful in our engagements, exemplary in our deportment, and to be zealous in our efforts to advance the kingdom of our Savior.

We further engage to watch over one another in brotherly love; to remember each other in prayer; to aid each other in sickness and distress; to cultivate Christian sympathy in feeling and courtesy in speech; to be slow to take offense but always ready for reconciliation, and mindful of the rules of our Savior to secure it without delay.

We moreover engage that when we remove from this place, we will as soon as possible unite with some other church where we can carry out the spirit of the covenant and principles of God's Word.

TYPE OF CHURCH COVENANT: C [1]

Having been led by the Spirit of God to profess our faith in Jesus Christ, and having been baptized in the name of the Father, the Son, and the Holy Spirit, we do now solemnly and joyfully affirm our covenant with God and with each other.

We pledge to serve Christ in the fellowship of this congregation. We shall endeavor to love one another, to remember one another in prayer, to share in each other's joys, and to sustain each other in times of distress. We aspire to be a fellowship of the concerned, where the lost may find Jesus Christ, sinners may find pardon, seekers may find meaning for their lives, and where all who come may find welcome. We shall strive to be responsible church members, through faithful attendance, study and giving.

We shall seek to be obedient to Christ in our daily living. Within our homes, in our labor, and while at leisure we shall strive for attitudes and actions which will reflect God's spirit working through us. Believing that our bodies are temples of the Holy Spirit, we shall endeavor to avoid experiences and habits which defile the body and hinder our witness.

Bound together in a fellowship of faith with all who confess Jesus Christ as Lord and Saviour, we shall pray and labor for a spirit of unity among all Christians.

Believing that our call to be a church is a call to witness in the world, we dedicate ourselves anew as servants of the Lord of all life. Whenever men are in bondage to ignorance, poverty, fear, or prejudice, we shall strive for justice, freedom, dignity and peace. Whenever men are separated by barriers of hostility and distrust, we shall be ministers of God's reconciling love. As we pledge our support to the work of our missionaries throughout the world, we commit ourselves to the mission to which God calls us all.

Acknowledging our human frailties and ever seeking forgiveness, we profess our need of the Holy Spirit, and commit our lives to Jesus Christ, and through Him to the care, the judgment, the deliverance, and the mercy of Almighty God. Amen.

[1] A description of the process by which this covenant was prepared appears in *Baptist Leader*, April 1966.

Appendix III

Suggested Constitutions for Baptist Churches

TYPE OF CONSTITUTION: A

ARTICLE I—Name

The name of this church shall be the ＿＿＿＿＿＿＿＿＿＿＿
Baptist Church of ＿＿＿＿＿＿＿＿＿＿＿.

ARTICLE II—Purpose

The purpose of this congregation is to give visible form to that faith and fellowship to which God has called his people. We acknowledge ourselves to be a local manifestation of the universal church in and through which Jesus Christ continues to minister to the world by his Holy Spirit. We shall seek to fulfill this calling through corporate worship services, through a program of Christian nurture by which our members may be built up in their faith and love, through proclamation of the gospel by word and deed, and through ministering to human need in the name of Christ.

ARTICLE III—Polity

Recognizing Jesus Christ as the only head of the church, this congregation shall seek to ascertain and to obey the will of our Lord in all matters of faith and practice. Authority to reach decisions for governing the spiritual and temporal affairs of this church being

216

given to us by Christ, we hold that such authority and responsibility is vested in the membership of the congregation.

In carrying out the wider ministry for which Christ has made his church responsible, we shall adhere to and be a member of the _____ Association, the _____ State _____ Association, the _____ State Convention, and the American Baptist Churches in the U.S.A. This church duly adopted amendment to the constitution of this church. No such action to amend the constitution shall take place until a consultation has been held by the boards of trustees and deacons of this church with the moderator of the association and the president (or executive secretary) of the state convention.

This church shall also be in co-operation with the larger Christian fellowship through the local and other councils of churches.

ARTICLE IV—Doctrine

This church accepts the Scriptures of the Old and New Testaments as the inspired record of God's revelatory actions in human history and as the authoritative basis for its doctrine and practice. The confession of faith drawn up and adopted by this church is regarded as an expression of the essential doctrines of grace as set forth in the Scriptures. This document shall be subject to revision by the congregation as new insights from the Word of God shall indicate ways in which our faith and life may be brought into closer accord with the teachings of Scriptures.

This church also has adopted the following covenant as a means by which its members may express their intent to accept the lordship of Jesus Christ in the life of the church and in the affairs of daily life:

[See Appendix II, pp. 207-209, concerning alternative covenants.]

ARTICLE V—Membership

Section 1. *Admission of Members.*—Persons may be received into membership by any of the following methods, subject in each case to the recommendation of the board of deacons and the vote of the church:

A. *By Baptism.*—Any person who confesses Jesus Christ as Savior and Lord and who is in essential agreement with the doctrine and practice of this church may be received into the fellowship of the congregation following his baptism by immersion.

B. *By Letter.*—A person who is in substantial accord with the doctrine and practice of this church may be received by letter of commendation from any other Baptist church.[1]

C. *By Experience.*—A believer of worthy character who has formerly been a member of a Baptist church and who, for a sufficient reason, cannot present a letter from that church but who is in substantial accord with the faith and practice of this church may be received upon statement of his Christian experience.[1]

D. *By Restoration.*—Any person who has lost his membership for any reason may be restored to membership upon recommendation of the board of deacons and vote of the church.

SECTION 2. *Dismissal of Members.*—Persons may be dismissed from membership by any of the following methods:

A. *By Death.*

B. *By Letter.*—Any member in good standing may receive a letter of dismission and recommendation to any other church, following the recommendation of the deacons and vote of the church. The name of the church to which membership is being transferred shall be named in the request and the letter shall be sent to the pastor or clerk of that church. Such letter

---

[1] Many churches admit persons from non-Baptist churches to full membership upon reception of a letter, or upon a statement of former Christian experience, when the deacons are satisfied that such persons manifest a genuine commitment of their lives to Christ. Such members have all the rights and privileges of the church, except that they may not serve as delegates to meetings of the American Baptist Churches in the U.S.A. (See pp. 80-86 for a discussion of the question of "open membership.")

Still other churches provide for associate membership. In such cases a person is received by letter or experience and is entitled to all rights and privileges of the church except that they are not allowed to vote on matters that determine the church's relationship to the American Baptist Churches in the U.S.A. Some churches place other limitations upon associate members, such as not allowing them to serve as trustees or deacons.

shall be valid for only six months after its date, unless renewed, and this restriction shall be stated in the letter.

C. *By Exclusion.*—Should any member become an offense to the church and to its good name by reason of un-Christian conduct, or by persistent breach of his covenant vows, the church may terminate his membership. Only after due notice and a hearing before the board of deacons, and after faithful efforts have been made to bring about repentance and amendment should such action be taken.

D. *By Suspension, or Erasure.*—The board of deacons should prepare annually, a list of members who have for a period of two or more years failed to participate in the public worship, the educational program, or the financial support of the church without valid reasons. If they are convinced that such persons cannot be reclaimed, they shall present to the church a recommendation that the names of these delinquent members be erased from the membership roll. Upon such action being taken by the church, said members shall thereafter cease to be members of this church.

ARTICLE VI—The Pastor and Officers

Section 1. *Pastor.*—The pastor shall be the leader of the church in all of its activities and shall preach the gospel, administer the ordinances, have charge of the stated services of public worship, and direct the spiritual welfare of the church. He shall be a member of all boards, committees, and auxiliary organizations of the church. He shall be elected by the church upon recommendation of the pulpit committee, as provided in Article VIII, Section 1.

Section 2. *Moderator.*—The pastor shall serve as moderator of the church and shall preside at all business meetings of the church and at all meetings of the advisory council.[2]

Section 3. *Clerk.*—A clerk shall be elected at each annual meeting to serve for one year. He shall keep a complete record of the transactions of all business at the meetings of the church. This shall

[2] Some churches have adopted the practice of electing someone other than the pastor as moderator. In that case, a moderator should be elected at the annual meeting to serve for one year. For discussion of this point, see pp. 59-60.

be read for approval at the next following business meeting. He shall keep a record of the names and addresses of members, with dates and manner of admission and dismission; also a record of baptisms and a list of those suspended, or erased. He shall notify all officers, committee members, and delegates of their election and appointment. He shall issue letters of dismission and recommendation voted by the church, preserve on file all communications and written reports, and give legal notice of all such meetings where such is required by this constitution. He shall also assist in preparing denominational reports. Immediately after the election of his successor, the clerk shall deliver to the new clerk all books and records for which he has been responsible.

SECTION 4. *Local Expense Treasurer.*—A local expense treasurer shall be elected at each annual meeting to serve for one year. He shall have custody of the funds of the church and all deposits made in the name of the church, and all checks drawn by him shall be in the name of the church. He shall keep separate accounts of all funds raised or contributed for particular purposes, and no funds shall be disbursed by him except for the purposes for which they were raised or contributed. He shall have custody of the securities, investments, title papers, and other valuable documents of the church.

Funds received for the support of the church, and for the reduction of the church indebtedness, shall be disbursed by him only on the order of the board of trustees.

He shall present to the church an itemized report of receipts and disbursements, showing the actual financial condition of the church at each annual meeting, this report to have been audited previously by the auditors elected by the church. He shall make such other financial reports as may be desired by the church.

He shall deliver immediately to his successor all books and records pertaining to his office.

SECTION 5. *Benevolence Treasurer.*[3] —A benevolence treasurer shall be elected at each annual meeting to serve for one year. He shall pay over, monthly, all funds received on account of the church's contribution to the benevolent purposes of the American

[3] In many smaller churches, the regular Treasurer serves also to handle all of the benevolence funds.

Baptist Churches in the U.S.A. and its agencies. Other benevolence funds shall be applied by him in accordance with the church budget and the special purposes for which the same were contributed.

He shall present to the church an itemized report of receipts and disbursements, showing the actual financial condition of the benevolence account of the church at each annual meeting, this report to have been audited previously by the auditors elected by the church. He shall make such other financial reports as the church desires.

He shall deliver immediately to his successor all books and records pertaining to his office.

SECTION 6. *Financial Secretary.*—A financial secretary shall be elected at each annual meeting to serve for one year. It shall be his duty to furnish each member of the church a pledge card and envelopes for contribution to church expense and benevolence; to keep a record of all pledges made; to collect all moneys contributed; and to keep a correct account thereof between the church and its members. He shall deposit such collections, weekly, in the bank selected by the board of trustees, and render a statement thereof to the treasurer. He shall, at the end of each fiscal year, report to the board of trustees an account of the matters pertaining to his office and report to the board of deacons the names of those members who have failed to make any contributions of record toward church expense or benevolence.

SECTION 7. *The Board of Trustees.*[4] There shall be a board of [3, 6, 9, or 12] trustees,[5] one-third of whom shall be elected at each annual meeting for a term of three years. No person may remain in the office of trustee longer than six consecutive years. He may be re-elected after a year has elapsed following the expiration of his period of service. The clerk, treasurer, and financial secretary shall have the privilege of attending meetings of this board, and shall be present when so requested by the board.

The board shall hold in trust all property belonging to the church and shall take all necessary measures for its protection, management,

[4] Under the alternate plan, providing for a central diaconate, the Board of Trustees will be constituted differently. See p. 223.

[5] Some states have legal requirements as to the number of trustees an incorporated church must have. It is desirable to consult an attorney on this and other matters which might be affected by state laws.

and upkeep. It shall determine the use of the church building by outside groups, and shall determine suitable charges to be made for such use. It shall designate the bank where the funds of the church shall be deposited, shall secure the services of a caretaker of the buildings at such salary as is authorized by the church and supervise his services, and shall transact all legal matters on behalf of the church.

The board shall supervise ways and means of raising the necessary funds for the support of the church and for the benevolences and for the disbursement of these funds as appropriated. It shall make written reports to the church at the annual meeting and at such other times as may be desired.[6]

The board shall arrange for an annual every-member canvass for the current expenses and benevolences of the church which shall be held in March or November. A representative committee shall be appointed to prepare a proposed goal for the every-member canvass. This proposal committee shall have representatives from the various boards and auxiliary organizations of the church. This proposed goal shall be presented to the church for adoption before the canvass. Following the canvass a budget of expenditures shall be set up by the board of trustees after consultation with the advisory council for adoption by the church at the annual meeting.

The board shall choose annually a chairman and a secretary and shall meet regularly each month. Special meetings may be called by the chairman or by the secretary, who shall notify the other members. A majority of the members shall constitute a quorum.

SECTION 8. *The Board of Deacons.*[7]—There shall be a board of [3, 6, 9, 12, or more] deacons, one-third of whom shall be elected from the membership of the church at each annual meeting for a term of three years. No person may remain in the office of deacon longer than six consecutive years. He may be re-elected after a year has elapsed following the expiration of his period of service. The

[6] This paragraph and the one following will apply to the work of a finance committee where the church does not assign such responsibilities to the board of trustees.

[7] An alternate plan for restoring to the diaconate responsibility for the whole life of the church is offered in Appendix B which immediately follows this suggested constitution.

board shall choose annually a chairman, a secretary, and a treasurer and shall meet regularly each month. Special meetings may be called by the chairman or the secretary, who shall notify the other members. A majority of the members shall constitute a quorum.

The board shall in every way assist the pastor in his work; consider with him all applicants for church membership and all requests for letters of dismission; co-operate with him in providing the pulpit supply and the leaders of the prayer meeting in his absence; visit the members; and care for the sick, needy and distressed members of the church, using such fellowship funds as may be needed.

The board shall promote Christian instruction and ministry to the church membership, provide for the Lord's Supper and aid in its administration; deliver to the treasurer the fellowship offering received at each communion service; and make a written report at each annual meeting of the church on the matters in its charge.

SECTION 9. *The Board of Christian Education.*—There shall be a board of Christian education composed of [3, 6, or 9] members one-third of whom shall be elected each year for a term of three years. No person who has served a full term shall be eligible for re-election for a period of one year following the expiration of his term of membership on the board.

The board shall be responsible for organization and administration of the entire educational program of the church. It shall be responsible for developing and interpreting to the constituency of the church the educational objectives or goals. It shall be responsible for studying the educational needs of the church and for making decisions concerning (1) time schedule, (2) educational use of housing and equipment, and (3) the elimination or addition of classes or organizations. It shall be responsible for discovering, enlisting, training, and appointing all church educational workers, subject to the approval of the church. It shall be responsible for evaluating and supervising the curriculum of the educational program. It shall be responsible for co-ordinating and approving the outreach programs of the groups and organizations under its jurisdiction. (Programs of home-church participation, community relationships, and educational activities in co-operation with other churches are included in this responsibility.) It shall be responsible for preparing and administering the education budget of the church.

The board shall be organized promptly following the annual election. It shall select from its own membership a chairman, vice-chairman, and secretary. It shall meet monthly at a stated time. Special meetings may be called by the chairman at any time and shall be called upon the request of the pastor. A quorum shall consist of_____elected members [usually a majority of the board]. The secretary of the board shall notify the members of all meetings, enter accurate minutes of the meetings in a book to be kept for that purpose, have custody of and be responsible for all books, papers, and documents pertaining to the affairs of the board, and surrender all records to the board when a new secretary is elected. The board shall prepare a report of the year's Christian education program, budget and activities for presentation at the annual meeting of the church.

SECTION 10. *The Superintendent of the Church School.*— At each annual meeting of the church a superintendent of the church school shall be elected for a term of one year. He shall be the executive head of the church school, exercising the authority and performing the duties usually pertaining to that office, following the general directives and policies of the board of Christian education.[8]

SECTION 11. *The Advisory Council.*[9]—There shall be an advisory council consisting of the elected officers of the church, chairmen of all standing committees, and presidents of all auxiliary organizations. All matters of importance should be considered by it before being presented to the church. It shall appoint, subject to ratification by the church, all standing committees. It shall seek to co-ordinate the activities of the church. It shall be instrumental in developing a program for the church.

[8] Where there is a director of Christian education employed by the church, it is sometimes considered appropriate that this person should serve as superintendent of the church school. This plan is not recommended, however, by the Board of Educational Ministries of the American Baptist Churches in the U.S.A.

[9] In some churches, the board of deacons serves as the advisory council. In that case, the diaconate would be enlarged accordingly, and the election of deacons would take into account the choice of persons suitable for serving on the various boards and agencies of the church. See the alternative constitution which follows on pp. 223-224.

ARTICLE VII—STANDING COMMITTEES

SECTION 1. *The Nominating Committee.*—The nominating committee shall be appointed by the advisory council within thirty days after the annual meeting. During the year, as vacancies in offices occur, it shall present suitable nominations for filling these. Prior to the next annual meeting, it shall prepare a list of those qualified to fill the various offices for which elections are to be held. It shall interview each nominee proposed and ascertain his or her willingness to serve if elected. The committee shall nominate one or more persons for each office to be filled, and report the names to the church at least one week before the election is to be held.

SECTION 2. *The Music Committee.*—The music committee, appointed by the advisory council, shall co-operate with the pastor in the selection of an organist and choir director and in the arrangement of the music of the church services. It shall incur expense only as authorized by the church.

SECTION 3. *The Ushering Committee.*—The ushering committee, appointed by the advisory council, shall attend to the seating of the congregation and to the receiving of the offering, except as otherwise provided.

SECTION 4. *The Auditing Committee.*—The auditing committee, appointed by the advisory council, shall audit the financial records of the church at least once each year and shall make a report in writing to the church at the time of the annual meeting.

SECTION 5. *Communications Committee.*—The communications committee, appointed by the advisory council, shall provide means by which the purpose and program of the church may be kept before the members and the community, such as bulletins, news letters, and the use of radio, television, and newspapers.

SECTION 6. *Committee on Christian Social Concern.*—The committee on Christian social concern, appointed by the advisory council, shall provide information, encouragement, and channels by which the lordship of Christ may be acknowledged, as it relates to social issues in the family, community, nation, and world.

SECTION 7. *Evangelism Committee.*—The evangelism committee, appointed by the advisory council, shall provide practical ways for implementing the evangelistic mission of the church, such as neighborhood visitation, preaching services, and study groups.

SECTION 8. *Committee on World Mission Support.*—The committee on world mission support, appointed by the advisory council, shall promote interest in missions and encourage their financial support. It shall co-ordinate its efforts with those of the committee on missionary and stewardship education of the board of Christian education.

SECTION 9. *Finance Committee* [See p. 216]. [In many churches the board of trustees serves in the capacity of a finance committee. If there is a separate finance committee, the material included in Article VI, Section 7, paragraphs 3 and 4 would be applicable here.]

ARTICLE VIII—*The Pastorate*

SECTION 1. *Calling a Pastor.*—When the pastorate is vacant, the advisory council [or board of deacons] shall select a representative pulpit committee of five or more members of the church. This committee shall take the necessary steps to secure the names of prospective pastors, working in full consultation with the Area Minister. It shall request from him full information about the record and qualifications of those persons whose names are submitted for their consideration, and the church shall not call a minister until such information has been so secured. When a suitable person is found for the pastorate, the committee shall recommend him to the church for consideration.

The call of a pastor shall be considered by the church at a regularly called meeting, notice of such meeting and its purpose having been read from the pulpit on two successive Sundays. A vote of three-fourths of the members present and qualified to vote, provided there be present and voting at least_____members, shall be necessary to extend a call.

Only one candidate shall be presented to the church at a time.

SECTION 2. *Termination of Pastorate.*—The term of office may be ended upon ninety days' notice on the part of the pastor or of the church.

Termination of the office shall be voted at a regularly called business meeting, notice of such meeting and its purpose having been read from the pulpit on two successive Sundays. A vote of a majority of the members present and qualified to vote, provided there shall be present and voting_____members, shall make valid termination of said office.

ARTICLE IX—Elections

SECTION 1. *Time.*—The annual election of officers shall be held during the annual meeting of the church, which shall be held on the second Wednesday evening in the month of _____.

SECTION 2. *Qualification of Voters.*—All matters pertaining to the purchase, sale, or mortgaging of property shall be voted on only by members in good standing and who are of legal age. On all other matters members in good standing who are fifteen years of age or older are entitled to vote.

SECTION 3. *Procedure.*—At least one week before the election the nominating committee shall present to the church the names of one or more persons for each office to be filled. At the time of the annual meeting it shall be the privilege of any member present and qualified to vote to place in nomination the name of any eligible person for any office not so nominated. A majority of the ballots cast is necessary for the election of any officer.

SECTION 4. *Vacancies.*—Vacancies occurring during the year may be filled for the unexpired term at any business meeting. The nominating committee shall present to the church nominees for the vacancy to be filled.

ARTICLE X—Meetings

SECTION 1. *Worship Services.*—Public services shall be held each Lord's Day, and the fellowship groups and the Sunday church school shall hold weekly meetings at a time to be fixed by the advisory council and approved by the church.

The Lord's Supper shall be observed on the first Sunday morning of each month, or at such other times as the church may determine.

Occasional religious meetings may be appointed by the pastor at his discretion, by the advisory council, or by the vote of the church.

SECTION 2. *The Church Meeting.*—The annual meeting shall be held on the second Wednesday evening in _____ for the purpose of receiving the annual reports of individual officers, boards and committees of the church and its auxiliary organizations; the election of officers; the transaction of necessary business; and the discussion of issues vital to the life and witness of the church. Quarterly meetings shall be held on the second Wednesday evening of _____, _____, and _____.

A quorum for the transaction of business shall be _____.

Special business meetings may be called at any time by the pastor or by the clerk. Notice of such meeting, and the object for which it is called, shall be given from the pulpit at least one week in advance of the date of the meeting. At any of the regular meetings of worship, however, the church may, without notice, act upon the reception of members, upon the dismission of members to other churches, and upon the appointment of delegates to councils, but not upon extraordinary business.

ARTICLE XI—CHURCH YEAR

The fiscal year of the church shall be the calendar year.

ARTICLE XII—AMENDMENTS

This constitution may be amended at a regular or called meeting of the church by a two-thirds vote of those present and voting, providing that a quorum is present and voting. Before such a vote can be taken, however, notice of the proposed amendment shall be sent to the moderator of the association and thirty days allowed for the association to offer any advice regarding the matter under consideration that it may wish to give. It shall also be necessary for the congregation to be notified by letter of the meeting and of the proposed amendment at least one month prior to the time when action is taken on the proposal.

TYPE OF CONSTITUTION: B

The following plan is offered as an alternate to the preceding constitution. Instead of a separate advisory council to serve as a coordinating agency, this pattern makes the board of deacons central and restores responsibility for the whole life of the church to the diaconate.[10] Such a plan is easily adapted to the needs of small con-

---

[10] For a discussion of the central diaconate, see pp. 113, 123.

gregations as well as larger ones, and it is being used in some American Baptist Churches in the U.S.A. churches.[11]

[Article I through Article VI, Section 6: the same as those in the preceding constitution.]

ARTICLE VI—The Pastor and Officers

SECTION 7. *The Board of Deacons.*—There shall be a board of [6, 9, 12, or more] deacons, three of whom shall be designated as trustees of the church property and authorized to sign legal papers at the direction of the church or the board of deacons. The deacons shall be divided into three classes of equal numbers, each class to serve three years, with terms of office so arranged that one class shall be elected each year.

The pastor and the board of deacons, subject to the approval of the church, shall direct all the various activities of the church in accordance with its purpose, polity, and doctrine as stated in Articles II, III, and IV. They shall be responsible for the services and meetings of the church, its program of Christian education, its evangelistic and missionary outreach, its witness to the community, the raising of funds, the care and maintenance of the property, and the administration of the finances of the church.

The board of deacons shall carry out its responsibilities through several committees. The various aspects of the work of the church shall be divided into [4, 5, or 6] departments, and a committee shall be responsible for each department. The chairman of each committee shall be a member of the board of deacons, but the other members of the committees may be drawn from the church at large and they shall be appointed by the board of deacons. In the election of deacons at the annual meeting, consideration should be given to the selection of persons who would be suitable to serve as chairmen of the several departments.

The board shall meet regularly each month, and at the first meeting after the annual meeting of the church, it shall choose a chairman, vice-chairman, and secretary. When the chairman of a particular committee cannot attend a meeting of the board of deacons, he may ask another member of the committee to attend in his place.

[11] The plan here proposed is adapted from the constitutions of the First Baptist Church, Oakland, California, the Normal Park Baptist Church, Chicago, Illinois, and the First Baptist Church, Chili, New York.

Each committee shall report its activities to the board of deacons each month and shall make recommendations for action by the board.

SECTION 8. *Nominating and Auditing Committee.*—In addition to the above committees of the board of deacons, the church at its annual meeting shall elect a nominating committee and an auditing committee to function for the ensuing year.

ARTICLE VII—DEPARTMENTS

SECTION 1. All activities of the church shall be assigned to the following departments: (1) department of evangelism and membership; (2) department of Christian education; (3) department of public worship (greeting, ushering, music, pulpit supply, flowers, etc.); (4) department of community relations; (5) department of finances; (6) department of property.

[The number of departments can be increased or decreased to meet the needs of the local congregation, but it is best to keep this number fairly small. The functions of all of the committees listed in the preceding constitution can be placed under one of the major departments. The size of each committee can be made large enough to take care of the duties which belong to a given department. In the rest of the sections under Article VII, the specific departments should be listed, the areas of responsibility assigned to each department stated, and the number of persons on the department committee given.]

[Articles regarding stated meetings, the church fiscal year, and the amending of the constitution will be the same as those in the foregoing constitution.]

Appendix IV

Suggested Constitution for an Association[1]

ARTICLE I—Name

ARTICLE II—Purpose

The purpose of this association shall be to promote the unity, growth, and outreach of its member churches, and to foster whatever else may serve to promote the interests of Christ in the world.

ARTICLE III—Membership

Section 1. Churches are to be received into this association by submitting a petition to the executive committee setting forth their desire to be admitted, their faith, practice, and willingness to cooperate fully and effectively with the American Baptist Convention, the _____ State Baptist Convention, and the _____ Baptist Association. The recommendation of the executive committee and a three-fourths vote of all delegates present and voting at a meeting of the delegates shall be required to receive a church into membership.

Section 2. This association shall have the right to terminate the membership of any church, when such church is out of harmony with established Baptist belief and practice or has withdrawn from the American Baptist Convention or has pursued a course inimical

---

[1] This constitution is an abridgement of that of the Monroe Baptist Association of Rochester and Vicinity. It was revised in April 1961.

to the good name of the association. The recommendation of the executive committee and a three-fourths vote of all delegates present and voting at a meeting of the delegates shall be required to terminate the membership of any church.

ARTICLE IV—Delegates

Each member church shall be represented at meetings of the association by three delegates, who shall be members in good standing in that church; its minister and two legally qualified additional delegates, elected by such church at its annual meeting. Churches with more than 500 members shall be entitled to one additional delegate for every 500 members or fraction thereof in excess of the initial 500 members. All officers of the association shall be delegates ex-officio, with full right to vote.

ARTICLE V—Meetings of the Delegates

Section 1. The delegates shall meet at least two times each year, at such time and place as shall be fixed by the executive committee. Such occasions shall be designated meetings of the association. The first meeting following the beginning of the calendar year shall be the annual meeting. The annual meeting shall be an open one, to which all members of the co-operating churches shall be invited without the right to vote. The executive committee shall call a special meeting of the delegates whenever so requested by five delegates representing at least five churches.

Section 2. One-fourth of the total number of delegates shall constitute a quorum for the transaction of business at any meeting.

Section 3. The delegates shall be the trustees of the corporation constituting this Baptist Association. They shall elect the officers of the association, the executive committee, the finance committee, the nominating committee, the officers of the permanent council on ordination, and the chairmen of divisions. They shall also establish other committees as may seem necessary, shall adopt rules and by-laws, shall alter and amend such rules and by-laws, shall be responsible annually for adopting a budget for the association, shall control all property belonging to the association, shall purchase, sell, mortgage, and lease real property in accordance with the laws of the State of ___, and generally shall exercise all powers and duties necessary for the proper management of the affairs of the association.

ARTICLE VI—Officers

SECTION 1. The officers of the association shall consist of a moderator,[2] a clerk, and a treasurer.

SECTION 2. The clerk shall be elected for a term of one year and may continue to hold office through re-election each year until a successor is elected. It shall be the duty of the clerk to keep a roster of the delegates elected or appointed by each church clerk, and to record the minutes of the meetings of the delegates.

SECTION 3. The treasurer shall be elected for a term of one year and shall continue to hold office through re-election each year until a successor is elected. It shall be the duty of the treasurer to keep all moneys of the association and to disburse them in accordance with the budget adopted at a meeting of the delegates or as subsequently amended and revised by a majority vote of the delegates; to make investments of the funds of the association at the direction of the finance committee; to keep an accurate record and to make such reports as the executive committee may require; and to transmit to his successor the books with all moneys and vouchers as shown thereby belonging to the association, and with which he is chargeable at the expiration date of his term of office. He shall receive and hold all deeds of property and all vouchers of payment made by him, and shall give a bond for such sum as the executive committee shall fix, the fee for which bond shall be paid by the association.

SECTION 4. A moderator pro tem and/or clerk pro tem, may be elected at any meeting at which the moderator and/or the clerk is absent.

[2] When an association has a full-time executive minister, he should be elected for an indefinite term by a three-fourths vote of all delegates present and voting at a meeting of the delegates, and he shall continue to serve unless removed from office by a majority vote of all delegates present and voting at a meeting of the delegates. The executive minister shall be regarded as the spiritual director and administrative officer of the association. It shall be his duty to preside at all meetings of the delegates, to report annually on the affairs of the association, and to be responsible for the supervision of its work.

ARTICLE VII—Executive Committee

Section 1. The executive committee shall consist of the officers of the association, the chairmen of divisions, and twelve additional elected members. One-third of the elected members shall be elected each year for a three-year term. No such additional elected member having served a full term of three years shall, for a period of two years, be eligible for re-election. Not more than two members of the executive committee shall be members of any one church.

Section 2. Ten members of the executive committee shall constitute a quorum for the transaction of business.

Section 3. The executive committee shall act for the association in the intervals between meetings of the delegates, except that the executive committee shall not have the power to reverse, modify, or change any action of the delegates. The executive committee shall report at each meeting of the delegates.

Section 4. The executive committee shall have power to appoint all members of committees in the various divisions and special committees which the delegates shall establish to carry out the purpose of the association, with the exception of the finance committee, nominating committee, and the permanent council on ordination. It shall also have the power to appoint other special committees as may be needed to conduct the work of the executive committee.

ARTICLE VIII—Finance Committee

The finance committee shall consist of the officers of the association and at least ten additional members elected by the delegates. This committee shall have responsibility for the financial affairs of the association; shall supervise the work of the treasurer; provide for an annual audit of the treasurer's accounts; and make whatever other recommendations may be necessary to a meeting of the delegates. Delegates may authorize the finance committee to direct the investment of funds, including the purchase and sale of securities.

ARTICLE IX—Nominating Committee

The nominating committee shall consist of seven members elected by the delegates. No person may serve for two consecutive years as a member of this committee. The nominating committee shall mail a list of its proposed nominees for officers, chairmen of divisions, and members of elected committees to all delegates of record at least two weeks prior to the meeting at which the election is to take place.

ARTICLE X—Permanent Council on Ordination

Section 1. The permanent council on ordination shall consist of all delegates from each church in this association, together with the moderator and clerk of the association.

Section 2. The permanent council on ordination shall receive and consider requests for ordination from the churches.

Section 3. To best fulfill its purpose to counsel and advise each candidate (ordinand), there shall be a subcommittee called the examining committee. This committee shall be composed of six ordained ministers elected by the permanent council who, at some time prior to the meeting of the permanent council, shall interrogate all candidates thoroughly regarding their doctrinal beliefs and shall give the council such suggestions and recommendations as may be indicated in the inquiry.

Section 4. The permanent council on ordination shall meet whenever requests for ordination are received. The candidate shall give an extemporaneous account of his Christian experience and call to the ministry and shall read a two-page condensation of his doctrinal statement. At no meeting shall more than four candidates be examined.

ARTICLE XI—Divisions

Section 1. The organization of the association for the purpose of conducting its work shall be structured in terms of divisions, with appropriate committees within each division. These divisions, when elected or appointed, shall supervise, plan, and conduct the work of the association in their various fields, reporting to the executive committee and to the delegates.

Section 2. Each division shall have a chairman, elected by the delegates of the association, whose duty it shall be to preside over the affairs common to the division. Chairmen shall be elected for one year.

Section 3. The moderator and chairmen of divisions shall nominate to the executive committee the chairmen of committees within the divisions. The term of office shall be for one year.

Section 4. The chairman of each division, in conference with the chairmen of committees embraced within his division, shall have the power to select from the American Baptist constituency the members of committees within the divisions of the association, with the exception of the finance committee, the nominating committee, and the permanent council on ordination. The number of members on each committee shall be determined by the delegates or the executive committee. All appointments shall be for one year.

Section 5. All committees, except the executive committee, shall be a part of the divisional pattern of the association.

ARTICLE XII—Amendments

This constitution may be amended at any meeting of the delegates by concurrence of not less than three-fourths of the delegates present and voting; provided that written notice containing the substance of the proposed amendment has been mailed to all delegates of record at least thirty days before the date of the meeting at which the amendment is to be acted upon.

Suggested By-Laws for an Association

ARTICLE I—The Associational Year

ARTICLE II—Roster of Delegates

ARTICLE III—Letters to the Association

Each member church shall send a letter to the association not later than the first day of the month of _____, each year, indicating the state of the church, calling attention to the items of oustanding interest, and enclosing a statisical report of membership and finances for the preceding year.

ARTICLE IV—Message to the Churches

At least once each year, the association shall adopt and address a message to the churches dealing with some matter of common concern for their consideration, with the request that the message be read to each church.

ARTICLE V—Divisions and Committees

Section 1. The organization of the association for the purpose of conducting its work shall be structured in seven divisions with appropriate committees within each division. These divisions shall be: (1) local church program, (2) church extension, (3) financial affairs, (4) associational affairs, (5) church co-operation, (6) ministry, (7) related organizations.

Section 2. The division of local church program shall consist of the following committees: Evangelism, social action, Christian education. The Christian education committee shall be composed of the following subcommittees: Children's work, youth work, adult work, missionary and stewardship education, leadership education, and student work.

Section 3. The division of church extension shall be responsible for the establishment of new Baptist churches and the development of existing ones in expanding suburban areas and other localities as needed.

Section 4. The division of financial affairs shall consist of the finance committee with sections on operating budget and mutual assistance fund as defined in the constitution (Art. VIII). The chairman of the finance committee shall be the chairman of the division of financial affairs.

Section 5. The division on associational affairs shall be composed of the following committees: Nominations, communications, message to the churches, and local church affairs.

Section 6. The division on the ministry shall be composed of a permanent council on ordination as defined by the constitution. The chairman of the division on the ministry shall be the chairman of the permanent council on ordination. When meeting as such council, _____ members shall constitute a quorum. All requests for the service of the council shall be presented to the officers of the council, who shall then determine the advisability of calling the council together. The council shall publish and distribute to the member churches rules of procedure to be followed in ordination, including resident membership of ordinands, their good standing in the church of their membership, their educational qualifications, the mode of examination (whether paper or oral or both) including synopsis of paper to be presented to the full council, their appearance before the council, and recommendations concerning the formal ordination service.

SECTION 7. The division on related organizations shall consist of: the _____ Council of American Baptist Women; the _____ Council of Baptist Men; the Baptist Home; the Baptist Ministers' and Wives' Fellowship; and the _____ Baptist Youth Fellowship.

SECTION 8. Other committees may be established by the delegates of the association or by the executive committee.

ARTICLE VII—Delegates to the _____ Baptist Convention

The association shall designate three (3) delegates from the churches of this association to serve also as representatives to the State Baptist Convention, one delegate to be designated to serve as a member of the nominating committee of that convention, a portion of the expenses to be paid by the association.

ARTICLE VIII—Amendments

These by-laws may be amended at any meeting of the association by a majority of the delegates present and voting, provided the amendment has been recommended by the executive committee.

Appendix V

Ordination Procedures

A pamphlet describing the regular steps leading to the ordination of a minister in the American Baptist Churches may be obtained from American Baptist Churches in the U.S.A., Literature Service, Valley Forge, Pennsylvania 19481.

Appendix VI

Steps in Calling a Pastor

A pamphlet which outlines the regular procedures which a pulpit committee should follow in securing names of prospective pastors and information about such persons may be secured from American Baptist Churches in the U.S.A., Literature Service, Valley Forge, Pennsylvania 19481.

Appendix VII

Forms and Blanks

Forms for letters of dismission, baptismal and membership certificates, requests for church letter, ordination certificates, and licenses to preach, as well as other useful forms, may be obtained from American Baptist bookstores. See the latest Church Supply Catalogue from Judson Book Stores.

INDEX

241